THE GREAT
HISPANIC HERITAGE

Jorge Luis Borges

THE GREAT HISPANIC HERITAGE

Isabel Allende

Jorge Luis Borges

Miguel de Cervantes

César Chávez

Roberto Clemente

Salvador Dali

Francisco Goya

Oscar De La Hoya

Dolores Huerta

Frida Kahlo

Jennifer Lopez

Gabriel García Márquez

José Martí

Pedro Martinez

Ellen Ochoa

Pablo Picasso

Tito Puente

Juan Ponce de León

Diego Rivera

Carlos Santana

Sammy Sosa

Pancho Villa

THE GREAT HISPANIC HERITAGE

Jorge Luis Borges

Tim McNeese

CHELSEA HOUSE PUBLISHERS
An imprint of Infobase Publishing

Jorge Luis Borges

Chelsea House
An imprint of Infobase Publishing
132 West 31st Street
New York NY 10001

Library of Congress Cataloging-in-Publication Data

McNeese, Tim.
Jorge Luis Borges / Tim McNeese.
p. cm. — (The great Hispanic heritage)
Includes bibliographical references and index.
ISBN 978-0-7910-9665-9 (hardcover)
1. Borges, Jorge Luis, 1899-1986. 2. Authors, Argentine—20th century—Biography. I. Title. II. Series.
PQ7797.B635Z7766 2008
868'.6209—dc22
[B] 2007032008

Chelsea House books are available at special discounts when purchased in bulk quantities for businesses, associations, institutions, or sales promotions. Please call our Special Sales Department in New York at (212) 967-8800 or (800) 322-8755.

You can find Chelsea House on the World Wide Web at http://www.chelseahouse.com

Text Design by Takeshi Takahashi
Cover design by Keith Trego and Jooyoung An

Printed in the United States of America

Bang EJB 10 9 8 7 6 5 4 3 2 1

This book is printed on acid-free paper.

Contents

Introduction

He was born under a curse. For the middle-aged Jorge Luis Borges, one of Argentina's most recognized and honored literary figures of the twentieth century, the world was becoming increasingly dark. Yet it was not in the same sense as with the many great authors who write about human tragedies but in a personal, physical way. Borges's tragedy was inherited. For generations, members of Borges's family had struggled as their vision failed, finding their view of everything growing dimmer with time until they were left to struggle in complete darkness.

A DARK FAMILY LEGACY

Blindness had plagued the Borges family for generations. His father, the elder Jorge Borges, always struggled with bad eyes. Knowing the potential danger to his son, he had not waited long to check his infant's eyes. Since blue eyes did not run in his family, he was ecstatic when he realized his newborn's eyes were blue. Excitedly, he told his wife, "He is saved. He has your eyes."[1] Unfortunately, he was wrong. He did not realize that all infants' eyes are blue. The infant Jorge's eyes would not remain blue. Jorge Luis would become the sixth generation of his family cursed with poor eyesight. For most of his life, he would experience the world on the edge of blindness.

It was a handicap that was made more unforgivable by the fact that earlier generations of Borges's family had made their mark in the world through their physical exploits and military careers. Earlier Borges men had been virile warriors. These ancestors were among the first Europeans to reach the Western Hemisphere to conquer the New World in the name of the Spanish crown. They had been hard, driven men of the world. They were explorers, conquistadors, provincial rulers, and the founders of imperial cities, who had laid the foundations of a Spanish empire. One had fought alongside Francisco Pizarro, the Spanish conquistador and conqueror of the vast Inca Empire of Peru. Another soldiered control of Paraguay for his Spanish monarchs. Yet another had established the city of Cordoba in Tucumán, a province in northern Argentina. Still another help found Buenos Aires, the Argentine urban center Jorge Luis Borges would make his twentieth-century home. Such men made up the legacy of the Borges family. There were times when their violent machismo made their modern-day descendant feel inadequate and inconsequential. Having poor eyesight simply rubbed salt into the wound.

MEN OF ARMS

The long list of family heroes sometimes seemed endless. For all those who had marched on behalf of the Spanish crown and conquered in its name, another generation of Borges's ancestors had fought *against* Spain to help establish freedom and independence for the nation of Argentina. On his mother's side, the family had descended from "a line of Argentine soldiers and freedom fighters."[2] The walls of her childhood house were decorated with reminders of those fighting ancestors.

Argentine-born Jorge Luis Borges (1899–1986) was a writer of short stories and fictional essays who also gained international fame as a poet, critic, and translator. In the span of his 60-year career, Borges created one of the most significant and lasting legacies of any writer of the twentieth century.

Jorge's mother, Leonor, had grown up in a middle-class family of Catholics. Her paternal grandfather, Francisco Narciso de Laprida, had fought for Argentine independence from Spanish colonial rule. He had even presided over the 1816 Congress of Tucumán, the Argentine equivalent of America's Second Continental Congress of 1776. Her father, Isidoro de Acevedo Laprida, had fought in an earlier Argentine civil war (1835–1852) against his country's heavy-handed ruler. Although Jorge Luis would know little about him (his grandfather died when Jorge Luis was only six years old) he would one day write a poem in his honor, titled "Isidoro Acevedo." Yet to write a poem and to found a nation were two endeavors worlds apart, and Jorge Luis Borges's words seemed puny to him compared to his ancestors' exciting military deeds.

The exploits of these maternal ancestors, however, stood in the shadows of Jorge Luis's great-grandfather, Manuel Isidoro Suarez. Born in 1799, he was a man of legend for having engaged in a cavalry charge at the age of 24. Suarez had led the charge that would be remembered as the Battle of Junin, the next-to-last military engagement in the liberation of South America from Spanish domination. The August 1824 battle was fought in the high country of the upper Andes Mountains of Peru where "the lofty silence of the snow-capped peaks was broken only by the clash of lance and sword, for no guns were used in combat by either army."[3] The entire engagement had taken only one hour, but the rebellious patriots brought about the defeat of the Spanish. Suarez's actions that day would be long remembered and even noted by one of the greatest liberators on the continent, Simón Bolivar. He would later note of Jorge Luis's great-grandfather that "when history describes the glorious Battle of Junin . . . it will be attributed to the bravery of this young officer."[4] Suarez further distinguished himself in the Battle of Ayacucho, the final fight to oust the Spanish, for which Bolivar promoted him to the rank of colonel.

Borges's father also had claims to a military past. Jorge Luis's grandfather, Colonel Francisco Borges, had died in battle in 1899, the same year his new grandson was born. The military lineage of the family was to remain only a legacy for both Leonor and Jorge Guillermo Borges. Their son would have nothing to do with swordplay, battles, dueling, or a soldier's death. These were scenes destined only for the pages of his writings. Of his ancestors, he would one day write, "On both sides of my family, I have military forebears; this may account for my yearning after that epic destiny which my gods denied me, no doubt wisely."[5] Instead, his world would be filled with books. Yet reading those favorite works would become increasingly difficult, if not impossible, as his eyes lost touch with the world around.

A DIM VIEW OF THE WORLD

Jorge Luis Borges could see where his vision problems would take him even before his eyes began to dim. He had watched his father lose his eyesight even as the younger Jorge was growing up. When he was 15 years old, he and his family had left their Argentine home for Switzerland. His father, then only 40 years old, was panicking about his vision—and for good reason. He was already beginning to lose his sight. There was an eye specialist in Geneva who offered surgery and much promise. It was 1914, and young Jorge Luis knew reasonably well that his father's eye problems would likely become his own in the future.

In the following years, his father went through further operations, but each brought only temporary relief. Before Jorge Luis himself would turn 40, his father died nearly sightless, an embittered man who had fallen into deep depression, refusing to eat or even take his medications. His father had struggled through decades with his poor eyesight, only to lose the struggle and die in darkness. By then, his son had seen an entire lifetime of eye disease comprised of the last half of his father's life and the first half of his own. His vision had

Borges's birthplace, Buenos Aires, is the capital of Argentina. This photo, taken in 1941, shows the city at about the time when he was first beginning to create his unique style of "Borgesian" fiction writing.

deteriorated so early that "he very rarely bothered to wear spectacles after childhood."[6]

By 1927, Jorge Luis went under the knife himself, as cataracts were already dimming his eyes. He was only 28 years old. Over the following 30 years, he would have four more eye surgeries. By 1956, he had eight surgeries. Yet nothing had helped. Darkness continued to tap him on the shoulder, and the words on the pages of books he loved were becoming increasingly dim. It was through these cherished books that Jorge Luis Borges had made a life for himself and a reputation as a writer of poetry, fiction, and critical essays. Books had always served as his compass in life, as the center of his being. While he was still a youth with no real understanding of the world, Borges had begun to read, to soak in the words that others had written about other worlds. His literary energies had directed him to a career as an author and critic, one who would read hundreds of volumes. He, in turn, had taken up his pen. His writings were destined to become symbols of the literary power of his Argentine homeland. He would become the voice of its history, the history that his own ancestors had helped direct.

Yet now, as a middle-aged man recognized for his words, the light was dimming. His career had arced to, perhaps, its highest peak. The family curse had followed him all his days. His father had gone blind. He had watched his grandmother lose her sight. Now it appeared was his turn. What would his future be? How could he continue his career as a writer? Would his descent into blindness end one of the most significant careers of a twentieth-century Argentine literary figure?

1

Argentine Son

Jorge Francisco Isidoro Luis Borges Acevedo came into the world prematurely, his mother only having reached the eighth month of her pregnancy. He was born August 24, 1899, in the home of his maternal grandmother. It was the birthplace of his mother 23 years earlier. The house, located on calle (street) Tucumán 840 in downtown Buenos Aires, is no longer there. (Today, a literary center dedicated to Borges stands on the site.) It was a simple structure, a single story with a high front facade. Inside the colonial-style house was a long entrance hallway and several interior patios, "with a well, a vine and water tank that even had turtles in it to keep the water free from mosquito larvae."[7] The house was similar to many others built in the capital of the South American nation of Argentina, one that the adult Borges would describe as "small [and] unassuming."[8] For all its humble lines, the adult Jorge Luis Borges would write poems about growing up in this traditional colonial house, even though the family would move to their own house when he was two years old.

DUAL INFLUENCES

His parents were Leonor Acevedo and Jorge Guillermo Borges, and they had married the previous year. They had known one another for five years prior to their marriage. Their union created a unique family tree. Its roots revealed a twisted, complicated lineage that included Argentine, Anglo-Saxon, Portuguese, and Jewish ancestors. The family's English roots dated back to Jorge Luis Borges's grandfather's marriage to an English woman, Frances Haslam, from Staffordshire, in England's ancient Northumbria region. The family would fondly remember her as Grandmother Fanny. She and her grandson, Jorge Luis, would become quite close. Borges would relate how his grandmother met the man who would become his paternal grandfather:

> It was in Parana, the capital city of Entre Rios, that Fanny Haslam met Colonel Francisco Borges. This was in 1870 or 1871, during the siege of the city by the *montoneros*, or gaucho militia of Ricardo Lopez Jordan. Borges, riding at the head of his regiment, commanded the troops defending the city. Fanny Haslam saw him from the flat roof of her house; that very night a ball was given to celebrate the arrival of the government relief forces. Fanny and the Colonel met, danced, fell in love, and eventually married.[9]

Fanny was a teller of stories, who "often entertained her grandson with tales about the frontier days and about his heroic grandfather."[10] It was a legacy that the adult Jorge Luis would be proud of. Yet Grandmother Fanny also gave her grandson another important connection, one that helped form him into the man he would become one day: she introduced him to English culture.

Jorge Luis was raised in a household of dual influences, Argentine and English. Both English and Spanish were spoken at home. The elder Jorge was a practicing lawyer and would-be writer and intellectual. He was also a student of modern languages and occasionally taught psychology classes to English-speaking students. His library at home contained more books by English writers than any other nationality. This great library of classical English works would have a unique impact on the young Jorge Luis. He would later write, "If I were asked to name the chief event in my life, I should say my father's library. In fact, sometimes I think I have never strayed outside that library."[11]

A FAMILY'S STORY

When Jorge and Leonor moved from her mother's house with their young son, they took residence in a house on calle Serrano in Palermo. Their first residence was at Serrano 2135, but they soon built a house of their own on Serrano 2147. (Although neither house exists today, the street has been renamed after Jorge Luis Borges, and the neighborhood is "a trendy area of restaurants, low houses and shady streets.")[12] This neighborhood was less than ideal, "an affordable and somewhat rough suburb on the northern outskirts of Buenos Aires that was notorious for its history of *compadritos* [hoodlums] and knife-fighters."[13] While the neighborhood was probably not as bad at the turn of the century as it had been in earlier years, stories of bloody knife fights and the doings of seedy characters were common and "influenced Borges's imagination,"[14] even if he never witnessed any actual violence himself. As the son of upper-class parents with intellectual tendencies, he led a sheltered life. Although he would one day describe his neighborhood as "a suburb of adventurous streets and visible sunsets," he was compelled to admit that he "grew up in a garden, behind a speared railing, and in a library of unlimited English books."[15]

Young Jorge Luis lived in Palermo, Argentina, until his mid-teens. Palermo, shown here in the 1920s, had once been a rough neighborhood, producing stories of dangerous hoodlums and seedy characters. These tales reportedly influenced Borges's developing imagination.

Life for the Borges family was simple during these years in their spacious, two-story house. A photograph of Leonor and the elder Jorge exists, revealing a handsome, well-off couple living life fashionably in early twentieth-century Buenos Aires. They would not spoil their son, however, for young Jorge grew up with an affection for simple ways. It was a lifestyle that he would take to his grave. In fact, the adult Jorge had "a scorn for wealth and luxury."[16] Even if the Borges were thriving, they were not rich. Leonor's family had at one time been wealthy Argentine landowners but had fallen on hard times, and they were forced to surrender most of their properties, making them *hidalgos pobres*, or the "shabby genteel." Such influences on the young Jorge would encourage him to keep all things simple throughout his life.

Jorge grew up in a loving family. They referred to him as "Georgie," a habit his mother never grew out of, even to her death at the age of 99. (Taking his cues from the traditions of a Victorian household, he called his parents the more formal "Mother," or in Spanish, "Madre," and "Father.") He was extremely close to his parents and enjoyed the company of his younger sister, Norah, who was born when he was two years old. The two siblings spent most of their time at home, having few other young friends or playmates. Young Jorge and Norah imagined invisible friends in place of no friends at all. They were nearly inseparable. They read together and created plays out of stories found in the pages of their father's books. Their mother's garden and their father's library were their sanctuaries.

No other young person would be as important to young Jorge Luis as his sister. They lived under the same roof for 15 years until young Borges left home to attend a private school in Switzerland. Norah was a self-determined young girl who was much more physical than her brother, as well as more dominant. Often, when they played games or worked up new fantasies, she would take the most important role, such as a queen, while her brother might only be a prince. She often picked the games and made up the rules or instructions. Jorge Luis merely followed her lead. According to their mother, brother and sister never argued about anything.

The Borges children had at least one other playmate. This was Esther Haedo, a second cousin on their mother's side. Her family lived outside the capital city of neighboring Uruguay. It was here that the Borges family sometimes spent their summer

JORGE LUIS'S EARLY FEARS

Every young child has his or her personal fears, such as the doubts and dreads that range from believing in a monster in the closet to a fear of dogs. Compared to the more frequent things that scare kids, such as the dark, spiders, or other common phenomena, Jorge Luis Borges had a few fears that might be considered very unusual.

As an elderly man, he admitted in his writings that he had always had a fear of such things as crystals, dark mahogany wood, and still, unmoving water, like that found in ponds and puddles. Why those three examples were reasons to instill panic in the young Borges is unclear and will probably never be explained. Yet the young Borges also had another fear, one that may have had a deeper psychological meaning altogether. He described it in 1970 as "being afraid of being repeated."* The problem seems to have begun with several mirrors that the young Jorge had in his boyhood room. He wrote, "I had three large mirrors in my room when I was a boy and I felt very acutely afraid of them, because I saw myself in the dim light—I saw myself thrice over, and I was very afraid of the thought that perhaps the three shapes would begin moving by themselves."** In the boy's mind, he was fearful of self-multiplication through these mirrors.

Perhaps the root of young Borges's problem lies in his boyhood discovery of his own face. Apparently, it was an experience that he did not enjoy. It seems that all through his life, Borges did not like his own appearance, and for his face and body to be repeated in a combination of mirrors was more than he could stand. As an adult, this irrational fear of "being repeated," of having an existence outside of himself by losing control of one's mind with drugs or alcohol, constantly terrified him.

* James Woodall, *Borges, A Life* (New York: BasicBooks, 1996), 15.

** Ibid.

months, from December to March. Esther's father, a cousin of Leonor's, lived in a suburban villa there. Esther, Jorge, and Norah were good friends who enjoyed spending time and having fun with one another. As children, they formed a secret society called "The Three Crosses." The three youngsters grew up to remain good friends as adults. During these stays in the Haedo household, Jorge would visit the local beach at Capurro, where he learned to swim. Although he was never skilled at sports or even interested in them, Jorge would always enjoy swimming.

Another place for the family was a summerhouse in the town of Adrogue, south of Buenos Aires. In the early years, the family lived in a rented villa. In later years, Jorge Luis would remember the house's gardens and the heavy scent of eucalyptus. Later, the elder Borges put up his family in a local hotel, the Las Delicias. From here, the family made regular visits to a local botanical gardens and zoo, which Jorge Luis loved. He especially enjoyed watching an Indian tiger, "an image that haunted much of his poetry and fiction."[17] It appears that he loved the zoo and the tigers so much that he often threw a tantrum when told he had to leave. His mother sometimes had to punish him for such bad behavior by locking him in his room or even taking away his book-reading privileges. These parent-child dramas were significant enough to cause Jorge Luis's mother to recall, "When we visited the zoo, it was difficult to make him leave. And I, who was small, I was afraid of him, so big and strong. I was afraid that he'd get into a rage and beat me. . . . However, he was very kind."[18]

HOUSE OF BOOKS

Curiously, despite Jorge Luis's intellectually driven and book-filled household, the young Jorge did not attend a single school until the age of nine. One reason appears to have been a fear that the Borges children would contract childhood diseases from their classmates. As an adult, however,

Jorge Luis believed there was another reason. As he would later write, the elder Borges was not only an intellectual lawyer, but he was also

> an anarchist, libertarian, and admirer of the English philosopher Herbert Spencer's teachings, [who] did not trust any type of state-run enterprise and did not want his children to be indoctrinated by the state's religion or nationalism. So, Borges's earliest education derived from his father, his grandmother Fanny, and his English nanny and tutor, Miss Tink.[19]

The result of his father's decision was an early education that pinballed young Borges from subject to subject and from book to book, much at the whim of young Jorge himself. Fortunately, he was a motivated student who loved reading books, even if he was nearsighted and had to wear glasses. If he was denied the real or alleged adventures of his bourgeoisie neighborhood, with its seedy taverns, tango dancers, gamblers, and prostitutes, he found enough adventures between the covers of his father's books, reading in both Spanish and English.

Borges read his first novel as a preteen. It was the American classic *The Adventures of Huckleberry Finn.* He followed that by reading *A Thousand Nights and a Night.* Other books followed, with many of the earlier ones being English and American works. His exposure to Spanish literature would come later. The young Jorge consumed books and poetry of English writers such as H.G. Wells, Robert Louis Stevenson, Charles Dickens, Lewis Carroll, Rudyard Kipling, Percy Shelley, John Keats, and Algernon Charles Swinburne. His American readings included works by the master of the macabre, Edgar Allan Poe; the novelist of the great Alaskan north, Jack London; and the poet Henry Wadsworth Longfellow. He also read the stories compiled by the German Brothers Grimm. The Spanish writers of his youth included the Argentine poet José Hernández, author of the epic poem *Martín Fierro.* He read the stories

Robert Louis Stevenson (1850–1894) was a Scottish novelist, poet, and travel writer whom Borges greatly admired. Among Stevenson's greatest works are *Treasure Island*, *Kidnapped*, *The Strange Case of Dr. Jekyll and Mr. Hyde*, and a collection of short stories, *The New Arabian Nights*.

spun by the Spanish writer Cervantes, especially *Don Quixote*, even if he read them in English, not Spanish. Young Georgie even read the Argentine equivalent of the American cowboy

Westerns. These were the tales of South American gauchos, who perhaps reminded him of the montoneros, whose siege of Parana had brought Grandmother Fanny and Colonel Borges together decades earlier.

This reading and adventure-seeking on the pages of his father's books were formative for the young Jorge. As one biographer described that influence: "Books were Borges's touchstone for reality, how he interpreted the world; reading was his first skill, his chief inheritance, and the foundation of a scattershot education."[20] The influences of these works were something Borges himself was keenly aware of as an adult. At the age of 70, he wrote, "that it was Huckleberry Finn and 'the *Quixote*' that stayed closest to him into old age."[21]

All this reading as a young boy led Jorge Luis to try his hand at writing. His mother later recalled that her son had stated at age six that he wanted to be a writer. Most of his writings that followed merely mimicked other stories he had read. Yet he did become a published "writer" at age nine when he translated into Spanish a story by British author Oscar Wilde that ran in the local newspaper *El Pais.* When he signed his first work as "Jorge Borges," many who knew his family thought the work had been translated by his father.

SCHOOL DAYS

When Jorge Luis was nine years old, his father finally relented and agreed to have his son educated in a more structured and academically complete environment. The experience brought a new reality to the young Jorge Luis Borges. At this school in Palermo, the other boys spoke Spanish and enjoyed sports and roughhousing. They did not understand young Borges. The adult Borges would write how different he was and how he stood out from the other boys as a "soft-faced, bespectacled, stammering boy in ridiculous clothing—an Eton collar and tie." The other boys soon saw him as "a mannerly boy who spoke English, dressed funny, did not like sports, and excelled in academics."[22] (His stammer remained a problem for Borges well into his adulthood.) The other school boys soon turned on him, making his life miserable by picking on him constantly.

In addition, the school did not seem to offer classes that were meaningful learning experiences for young Jorge. It seemed sometimes that the school only taught civics lessons on how to be a good Argentine citizen and how to appreciate the great names of Argentine history, such as the nation's liberator, José San Martin. Yet he learned to fend a little better for himself, while learning the new words of the streetwise slang, the *lunfardo*, common among Buenos Aires youth. He did show his teacher, Señor Aguero, that he was a good writer. Aguero is said to have noted, "The best essay is always his."[23] Jorge Luis attended secondary school a few years later, and the experience seems to have been slightly better. He did have a friend, Roberto Godel, from France, but little is known about him. The adult Borges never wrote about Godel. Borges attended this school, the Colegio Nacional Manuel Belgrano, for only a year.

Borges continued to learn at home from his father. Elder and younger Borges talked about philosophy, and his father was always teaching Jorge Luis new things to stimulate his mind. They played chess together and worked on mathematics. The household regularly hosted family friends and guests, including poets and writers. Perhaps the most frequent visitor to the Borges household was a second-rate poet, a friend of the elder Jorge's, Evaristo Carriego. At times, he lived with the Borgeses. He often came on Sunday afternoons, "after the [horse] races to talk and share a glass or two with Jorge."[24] The poet had a strong enough influence on young Borges that Luis would one day write a monograph about him, titled *Evaristo Carriego*, which was published in 1930. In the essay, the adult Borges wrote about Carriego's career as a poet and his death at age 29, in 1912, of tuberculosis. Borges remembered that the poet had once written a poem dedicated to

Borges's mother, Leonor, and had included a few lines about young Jorge Luis: "And may our son . . . go forth, led by the trusting wing of inspiration, to carry out the vintage of a new annunciation, which from lofty grapes will yield the wine of Song."[25] The words had been written in 1909, when Jorge Luis was only 10 years old. They were words that would one day seem prophetic.

2

Off to Europe

In 1914, the world witnessed the opening volleys of the European conflict that would one day be known as World War I. That same year, the elder Borges made a fateful decision for his family. They would move to Europe. In part, the move was driven by Jorge Luis's father's diminishing eyesight. Just three years earlier, his vision had become so poor that he had little choice but to retire from work, unable to effectively practice law. That summer, he was 40 years old and desperate. He knew of a famous eye doctor in Geneva, Switzerland. The doctor could perform an operation on the elder Borges's eyes and, hopefully, his vision might improve, or at least, stabilize. When the decision was made to move, everyone in the family was excited. Jorge Borges had enough put away in savings, plus his pension, to allow his family to establish themselves in Europe. He and Leonor would travel around Europe, while the two children would attend school in Geneva. (Switzerland was neutral and not fighting in the war.) For the 15-year-old Jorge Luis, leaving Argentina would be a relief from school bullies. What he could not have known at the time was that the move to Europe "would serve as an important catalyst in his development as a writer and intellectual."[26]

LIFE IN SWITZERLAND

The family took 10 days to pack everything they would need. Then, they set sail for England on a German steamship. Jorge rented out their home in Palermo with every intention to return some day. A formal family portrait was taken at a studio just before the Borges left on their journey. In it, the family is dressed in their best: the men in heavy topcoats and the women wearing coats, fashionable hats, and furs. Everyone appears adequately prosperous, yet middle-class. They are a handsome family, even if their faces appear a little sad. After a short visit in England, they stopped in Paris, and finally, traveled on to Geneva. Leonor's mother, Leonor Suarez, traveled with the Borges. Because the family reached Switzerland before the opening of the fall school term, Jorge Luis and Norah were tutored that summer in French. Norah excelled at it. Jorge Luis was less accomplished, but he had to learn the language because all the classes at the school he was to attend were taught in French.

In the meantime, their parents continued their European tour. The plan was to stay in Europe for a year. Other events, however, would soon interfere with the family's plans. The Borges had arrived in Geneva in mid-April. Within a few months, international rivalries and antagonisms across the European continent led to war. By August, from Russia to Austria and England to Germany, Europeans were fighting each other. For the elder Jorge and Leonor, the war immediately interrupted their travel plans. Their European tour was cut short in Munich, Germany, and immediately they began having problems returning to Switzerland. Fortunately, they

Borges lived on this street in Geneva, Switzerland, from 1914 until 1918. At that time the Borges family moved to Lugano, about 100 miles (161 km) away. During the later years of his life, Borges returned to live in Geneva, where he remained until his death in 1986.

were not European-born, but Argentines, and they managed to get back to Switzerland. Yet they were surrounded by the war and were forced to remain in Geneva for the next four years, until the conflict was over.

School became the center of life for Jorge Luis and Norah. They attended separate schools, bringing an end to their long relationship that had hinged for so many years on mutual play, imaginative games, and shared sibling experiences. They saw one another because they did not live at their schools. Instead, they lived with their parents in an apartment in the old part of the city. The teenaged Jorge was sent to College Calvin, a day school for boys. Norah attended the Geneva School of Fine Arts.

A NEW START

Jorge Luis's school days in Geneva were a stark contrast to his schooling in Palermo. Gone were the bullies, and young Borges found himself making many friends. In later years, he would write, "The first fall—1914—I started school at the College of Geneva, founded by John Calvin. It was a day school. In my class there were some forty of us; a good half were foreigners. The chief subject was Latin, and I found out that one could let other studies slide a bit as long as one's Latin was good."[27]

Also, the classes actually gave him opportunity to stretch his intellect. They were challenging because they were taught in French, which proved a bit difficult at first for Jorge. When he failed his first French examination, his schoolmates rallied behind him and petitioned the school to promote him anyway to the next grade level. This prompted the headmaster to relent and promote the boy. This experience was an important one for Jorge Luis. His friends had fought for him, something he had never known before. Also, he gained a new level of personal confidence.

While being different in school in Palermo had made Jorge Luis a target to the school's toughs and rascals, being different in the Calvin School was the norm. Many of the boys were from foreign countries. Among them, young Borges made two good friends, both of them Polish Jews, Simon Jichlinski and Maurice Abramowicz. They would become successes as adults, the first becoming a lawyer and the second a doctor. Borges recalled in later years how he had taught them both to play the card game, truco, "and they learned so well and fast that at the end of our first game they left me without a cent."[28] With these two new friends, Borges could share a drink and engage in long talks about literature. While both boys were important companions to Borges during his school days, Abramowicz, especially, would become a lifelong friend.

To help him in his studies in French, young Borges almost immediately subscribed to a French circulating library. Soon, he was swamped with French literature, which "became the second most important of his youth."[29] After English literature, the French works Borges came into contact with helped to shape his future writings. He read French poets, essayists, short story writers, and novelists. He read works by Gustave Flaubert, Émile Zola, and Guy de Maupassant. He struggled through Victor Hugo's *Les Miserables*, finding the book to be "so terribly emphatic,"[30] although he loved Hugo's poetry.

Through his years at the College Calvin, Borges achieved a full education. While literature and philosophy were important studies for him, the curriculum at Calvin included science and mathematics courses, including algebra, chemistry, physics, mineralogy, botany, and zoology. His mind was being stimulated at every turn. He studied new authors and philosophers, and he finally conquered the French language as well as German and Latin. During his first year of study at Calvin, he read English authors G.K. Chesterton and Thomas Carlyle, whose works "dazzled and also bewildered" him.[31] Chesterton would become one of his favorites and remain so for the next 20 years. He took classes in symbolist literature, and he read the works of Arthur Rimbaud and Stéphane Mallarmé. He read German expressionist poetry and reveled in avant-garde art. Decades later, he explained to a friend the importance of these years in Switzerland, saying, "Geneva was like home, a city that he knew better than Buenos Aires because of its natural size, and because he was young there."[32]

ADOLESCENT STRUGGLE

Not all of young Borges's experiences in Geneva would be literary. At least one would have lasting impact on him, leaving a permanent mark on his personal psychology. The teenaged Jorge Luis began to consider the opposite sex and his own sexual attractions. His father, who was often unfaithful to Leonor, asked his son one day if he had ever been intimate with a woman. When Jorge Luis told him he had not, the elder Jorge immediately arranged for his son to visit a local prostitute. The son dutifully went to the arranged meeting, but things went badly, and young Borges emerged from the incident psychologically damaged concerning sex. So traumatized was he that "he did not explore sexual relations again for another thirty years."[33]

There would, however, be other events that would work out a bit better for him. That same year, 1917, Jorge Luis and Norah were thrilled when their grandmother, Fanny Haslam, came to Geneva to stay with them. She had missed them in Argentina, and so she braved an ocean crossing, onboard a passenger liner, the same kind that were constant targets for German submarines. The children thought her quite brave for risking such a trip. Yet the gain of one grandmother was counterbalanced by the death of another. Not long following Fanny's arrival in Geneva, Leonor Suarez died in early 1918, at the age of 81. She was buried in Geneva.

In April 1918, the family moved to Lugano, more than 100 miles (161 km) east of Geneva, on the border between Switzerland and Italy. Their residence was the Hotel du Lac. The elder Borges had enough money to keep his family in Europe for another year. He was also maintaining his visits to his eye doctor, and the surgery had improved his eyes somewhat. With the move, young Jorge was unable to take his

Borges *(first person on left, top row)* attended Calvin College in Geneva, where he learned several languages and studied math, science, and philosophy. He was also introduced to the works of new authors, such as Thomas Carlyle and G.K. Chesterton.

degree at the Calvin School. Instead, he finished his baccalaureate degree at a school in Lugano. There, Jorge Luis and his sister reconnected with one another as they had not been able to do in Geneva because they attended different schools.

Life in Lugano was not an easy one for the Borges family. Switzerland had been able to avoid direct involvement in the war, but it suffered from food shortages similar to those in European countries that were at war. Suddenly, the war had caught up with the Borges. In later years, Jorge Luis wrote, "I had never experienced hunger except in the last year of World War I. . . . I remember that we thought [then] that the only thing we wanted was a little more bread, or one extra grain of rice."[34]

Even as his formal schooling came to an end, at least for the moment, Jorge Luis's studies did not. In August, for his nineteenth birthday, he asked for a German-English encyclopedia. Free to write what he chose, Jorge put his hand to playing around with English and French sonnets. None of these survive today, and the content of them is unknown, although he would later describe them as "poor imitations of Wordsworth."[35] It was during the family's stay in Lugano that Jorge Luis made an important decision about his writing. With his father's input, he decided to write primarily in Spanish, not in English or another of his secondary languages.

In fall 1918, the war finally came to an end. The four-year-long conflict concluded with the defeat of Germany, along with its allies that included the Austrians and Turks. The two sides agreed to an armistice that took effect on November 11 and, with the end of hostilities, the Borges family had the option again to return to Argentina. However, their decision would be based less on events in Europe and more on new circumstances in Argentina. Within two months of the armistice in Europe, Buenos Aires was being rocked by street riots brought on by contentious political issues.

A decision to leave Switzerland was made, however, and that spring the family moved to Spain. The move was made for several reasons. It was, after all, the country from which the majority of their ancestors had come. They would easily find a place for themselves among other Spanish-speaking peoples. Also, it would provide the elder Jorge with an opportunity to "educate himself, and above all his children, in the values of the old country."[36] They first took a train to Barcelona, in

Spain's Catalonia region. This was followed by a ferry trip to the island of Majorca, where they stayed for about 10 months, from March to December 1919. In the city of Palma, the elder Jorge put up his family in the Hotel Continental. Life in the city was cheap, since few foreign tourists went there. Other Latin Americans were there, however. In his autobiography, Borges recalled how "Spain at that time was slowly being discovered by Argentines."[37]

AN EARLY MENTOR

During their stay in Spain, the Borges men stayed busy with their literary endeavors. The younger Borges found new friends, several who were poets and enjoyed literature. He was still reading constantly and studying Latin. He was also writing poetry and youthful essays, and he was submitting works for publication, with various results. Jorge Luis sent a short story about a werewolf to a Madrid magazine, *La Esfera,* and it was rejected. He also sent a book review to a Geneva paper, the French-language *La Feuille,* and it was accepted. Jorge Luis had not actually submitted the piece himself. He sent it first to Abramowicz, who was in Geneva, who in turn sent it to the editor at *La Feuille.* The elder Borges was at work on a novel. (When he finished it in 1920, he personally paid for 500 copies to be printed.)

Jorge Luis spent a good deal of time swimming at various local beaches. Now 20 years old, he had honed his swimming skills to a much greater level than the average European of his day. Swimming was not particularly popular in Europe then and was certainly not as important an activity as simply visiting the beach to take in the sunshine and fresh air. Children were usually the only ones who ventured along the wet sand of the beach. To swim as skillfully as Jorge Luis claimed he could at that age would have set him apart from nearly everyone else.

By Christmas 1919, the Borges family moved again. This move was to Seville, one of the three most important cities in

Spain's Andalusian region, along with Granada and Cordoba. They did not remain there long, but Jorge Luis was able to take up with the local writers and poets, and he managed to get one of his poems published in a local journal, *Grecia*. It was his first published poem, a piece meant to sound much like Walt Whitman. These connections with writers, starving poets, and attention-seeking essayists was formative for young Borges. It would not be until his family made another move, this time to the Spanish capital of Madrid, that he found and joined a literary group that fed his soul, sparked his imagination, and "challenged his thinking about literature."[38] Chief among this group of literati in Madrid was an Andalusian poet, Rafael Cansinos-Assens.

BORGES DISCOVERS WALT WHITMAN

While new discoveries and intellectual insights became routine for the teenaged Borges once he arrived at College Calvin, he was most dramatically influenced by his discovery of the works of an American writer and poet, Walt Whitman. Borges read his first work of the nineteenth-century writer in German. Excited, he found a copy of *Leaves of Grass,* also in German. He then ordered a copy in English from London, bound in green, "and thereafter never put it down, nor left the poet behind."*

Nothing at the time had a greater literary and personal impact on young Borges than Whitman. Even 15 years later, Borges was able to write, "His power is so dominating and so clear that a mere glimpse shows us how powerful he is."** The American poet's words would become the epitome of literature to Jorge Luis. He was such an admirer of Whitman that he became, as one writer has described him, "a Whitmaniac."***

Young Borges connected with Whitman's magical words, and, from them, he took new meaning for his life. Whitman wrote of events and places in America, a country Borges had never visited. Yet that did not matter. He still gloried in

Cansinos-Assens became one of Borges's early mentors and inspired him as no living writer had to date. While Jorge Luis was capable of writing and speaking as many as a half dozen languages, Cansinos-Assens had command of 11. (Borges biographer Jason Wilson puts Cansinos-Assens's accomplished languages at 16.) He was already known for having translated *Arabian Nights* as well as the works of the German writer, Johann Wolfgang von Goethe, into Spanish.

The Andalusian had qualities that drew Borges to him almost immediately. He was 16 years older than Borges and had studied for the priesthood, but, after some investigation, he decided that he was descended from Jewish ancestors. In the early twentieth century, Spain was not a place that typically

Whitman's words. To him, Whitman was a shining example of "the vehemence of pride and audacity of freedom necessary to loosen the mind of still-to-be-formed America from the folds, the superstitions, and all the long, tenacious and stifling anti-democratic authorities of Asiatic and European past."[†] It was this intellectual freedom and rebellion from the rigid thinking of Whitman's that would provide such an important foundation for Borges and help form him into the writer he was to become one day.

Borges biographer, James Woodall, summed up the impact that Whitman had on Jorge Louis, writing, "Georgie believed the poet was speaking directly to him. He elevated him beyond the status of mere hero: Whitman became a household god, something to dream about and worship."[††]

* **James Woodall, *Borges, A Life* (New York: BasicBooks, 1996), 30.**

** **Ibid.**

*** **Jason Wilson, *Jorge Luis Borges* (London: Reaktion Books, 2006), 37.**

† **Woodall, 30.**

†† **Ibid., 31.**

opened its arms to Jews. Borges had already made friends with other Jews and was not put off by Cansinos-Assens's alleged ancestry. In addition, his would-be mentor was extremely tolerant of young, budding writers. Borges would later describe Rafael as "refined, equable, with the ardor of a poet restrained by a fortunate intellectual coolness, carrying a classical culture of Greek philosophers and oriental troubadours which attached him to the past, causing in him a love of notebooks and folios, unimpaired by modern marvels."[39] Borges was especially impressed with Cansinos's book collection:

> Once, I went to see him and he took me into his library. Or, rather, I should say his whole house was a library. It was like making your way through a wood. He was too poor to have shelves, and the books were piled one on top of the other from floor to ceiling, forcing you to thread your way among the vertical columns.[40]

To someone who had grown up with books seldom out of reach, Cansinos's house must have seemed like home to Borges.

Almost every Saturday night, Cansinos-Assens would preside over a group of 20 or 30 young poets and writers who met at the Café Colonial in Madrid to talk about literature. Cansinos referred to them all as his "disciples." Like Borges, nearly all of them felt stronger connections to European culture in general than with Spanish specifically. They all loved American jazz. Rafael would usually provide the topics for discussion. The group talked about everything from Parisian fads to free-verse poetry. They generally disdained "all that was typically Spanish from flamenco to bull-fighting."[41] From these literary sessions, a movement known as ultraism took root. (Although Borges claims that Cansinos coined the term "ultraism," it actually developed originally outside of Spain.) Ultraism "concerned itself with manifesto, attitude, and ideas. [It] focused on purity of metaphor and rhythm, and its creed celebrated the future and the new."[42] Its supporters believed in anarchy and free thought, and they did not believe in war. Borges became caught up in the movement, writing several poems and essays in support of its beliefs. He even drew his sister, Norah, into the movement. Already an artist, she made several woodcuts that adorned the covers of ultraist publications.

Borges wrote two books while living in Spain in the years directly following World War I. One was titled *Gambler's Cards*, which was a collection of essays. The other was a book of poetry that he titled either *The Red Psalms* or *The Red Rhythms*. (Years later, Borges could not remember which.) These poems were largely tributes to "the Russian revolution, the brotherhood of man, and pacifism."[43] Some of the poems survive today because they were published previously in magazines and journals. Borges, however, would not allow these works to survive. By the time he left Spain, he destroyed them, embarrassed at these products of his youthful writing career.

While such influences as Cansinos and the ultraists would have a dramatic and formative impact on Borges, he would not remain in Madrid or even Spain for much longer. He and his family made the decision to return to Buenos Aires after seven years of absence. By spring 1921, they were on their way. Jorge Luis was 21 years old and certain that his destiny was to write poetry and that Spanish would be his literary language.

3

The Busiest Decade

Twenty-one-year-old Jorge Luis was only 15 when he and his family left Buenos Aires for a one-year trip to Europe. They had passed seven years in exile, in part, due to the war. The Borges family had changed during those years away from Argentina. They had come to appreciate and even thrive in their various European cities of choice, perhaps none more than Jorge Luis. All four were sad to leave Spain and apprehensive about returning to their native land. They sailed on the liner *Reina Victoria Eugenia*, reaching Buenos Aires about late March 1921. In many ways, the younger Jorge was returning to a country and a city he knew little about. He had been protected as a youth and had rarely left the family compound, except for a few miserable years of schooling, and those had been spent in Palermo, not Buenos Aires. How would this land of his birth fit into his plans of becoming a professional writer?

A NEW CITY

The Buenos Aires the Borges family returned to was a different city than the one they had known in earlier years. It was now a city of two million inhabitants. It was also a wealthy city. It was experiencing change and the excitement of the new and modern, including new businesses, factories, and industries, especially mining and oil. Agriculture was booming, and the nation's postwar economy was growing by leaps and bounds. This productivity and economic development had already lured many immigrants to Buenos Aires. Politically, change was also taking place. Old Buenos Aires, as well as Argentina in general, had been ruled by large and powerful landowners who were backed by the military. Yet pressures had come to bear during the previous 30 years that had led to universal male voting rights for those 18 years and older. The Radical Party had been swept into power just a couple of years after the Borges had left and was still in power when they returned. The party had helped introduce free public schools. For nearly everyone, jobs were available during these boom years.

For the budding writer, a job was not in his plan, other than the work he might accomplish as an enterprising author. In this, he found complete support from his parents. There would be no "starving artist" period in the career of Jorge Luis Borges. The family was still relatively well-off. When they returned to Buenos Aires, the elder Jorge continued to rent out his house on calle Serrano and established his family at a new house at calle Bulnes 2216, near the heart of the city. As with the house in Palermo, this new residence was not in an enviable neighborhood. It was, in fact, "dominated by an enormous penitentiary, the area was full of beer factories, butchers and sleepy bars."[44]

It was here that Jorge chose to settle his family. He and Leonor did not expect their son to get a regular job. He was going to be a writer. This meant that Jorge Luis did not have to leave home and strike out on his own to find himself as an artist. Actually, he seemed in no hurry to leave home at all. His parents would continue to see to his needs. He could hardly cook for himself, and, while still in his twenties, his mother bought all his clothes for him. Getting away, out of the house, cutting himself off from family and familial supports never occurred to young Jorge Luis. "Jorge and Leonor were his keepers and, in effect, his pay-masters."[45]

While his family life continued as usual, young Borges found it difficult, at first, to adjust to Buenos Aires. He felt stifled and complained that the city had no literary pulse or life. He was bored with his new Bulnes neighborhood. He missed his old comrades who had gathered on Saturday nights to talk about literature and everything that interested them. His initial response, however, was premature. The city he now made his home had a rich culture all its own. The downtown center of Buenos Aires during the 1920s "was . . . very smart, with wide, jacaranda-lined boulevards, glossy shops, endless restaurants and bars, and high, elegant facades in the fashionable *style francais*: . . . a city . . . bursting with a sense of its own importance."[46] Buenos Aires did have opportunities to offer Borges. He just had to go out and find them—and find them he did.

Borges began a habit that he would continue for more than 30 years: "Walking endlessly along Buenos Aires streets, covering enormous distances, alone or with friends, musing and perhaps sketching poems or articles in his mind, talking about anything that took his fancy."[47] The city he had never really known was destined to become a city he would *learn*. It became to him the same that New York City's Manhattan Island became for Walt Whitman: the city he loved, the city that inspired him. Fifty years after his return to the city, Borges wrote, "The city—not the whole city, of course, but a few places in it that became emotionally significant to me—inspired the poems of my first published book, *Fervor de Buenos Aires*."[48]

Walt Whitman (1819–1892) was a poet, essayist, and journalist whose literary and personal impact on young Jorge Luis Borges was immeasurable. Among Whitman's most notable works are two collections of poetry, *Leaves of Grass* and *Drum-Taps.* He also published a collection of newspaper articles and other material, *Memoranda During the War*, which focused on the fighting spirit of soldiers in the American Civil War.

LITERARY FRIENDS

Through his years in Europe, Jorge Luis had learned to cultivate friends, especially those who had literary interests. Throughout the 1920s and 1930s, he made new friends in Buenos Aires too. Jorge Luis began putting together a literary magazine called *Prisma,* or *Prism,* with several of these new artistic associates. It was an effort that amounted to only two issues making it into print between December 1921 and March 1922. *Prisma* was intended as an ultraist publication. In fact, it really did not take the form of a true magazine at all. The project's organizers did not have enough money for expensive printing costs, so they worked out an inventive alternative. As Jorge later described, "Our small ultraist group was eager to have a magazine of its own, but a real magazine was beyond our means. I had noticed billboard ads, and the thought came to me that we might similarly print a 'mural magazine' and paste it up ourselves on the walls of the buildings in different parts of town."[49] Once the issues of *Prisma* were printed (they included woodcuts by Norah), Jorge and his handful of literary associates ventured out "armed with paste pots and brushes provided by my mother, and, walking miles on end, slapped them up along Santa Fe, Callao, Entre Rios, and Mexico streets."[50] To Jorge and his friends, it was all very modern, very alternative, very street-level available, and very avant-garde.

The thematic thrust of Jorge's *Prisma* was to preach the ultraist idea that traditional poetry relied too heavily on old, overused symbols or wallowed in self-analysis or autobiography. It was critical of long works, including overly elaborate novels and lengthy poetry, noting "that to achieve one good, valid verse the traditionalists write a whole sonnet or take two hundred pages to say what could be said in two lines."[51] In place of such out-of-date approaches, the ultraists writing in *Prisma* argued that writing needed to be freed from the approaches of the past and concentrate on one simple construct, the metaphor. (A metaphor is a figure of speech in which a word or phrase that usually designates one thing is used to designate another, such as "a sea of troubles" or "drowning in money.")

Decades later, after Jorge Luis Borges had lived long enough to discount much of his earlier ultraist agenda, he commented on the limited impact of *Prisma*: "Most of our handiwork was torn down by baffled readers, almost at once."[52] Perhaps the most positive impact of the magazine was that the first issue was noticed by Alfredo Bianchi, the editor of a more traditional literary magazine, *Nosotros (We)*. He asked Jorge to write a piece explaining exactly what ultraism was and what it hoped to accomplish. In a December 1921 article, Borges explained the importance of the metaphor in writing. He argued for the need to be precise, and even spare, when presenting literary ideas. Borges also noted that prose and poetry should be stripped of its nonessentials, such as overadornment and vague references that lack specificity. Yet beyond the heart of the explanatory piece about ultraism, Jorge's essay represented an important opportunity for Jorge Luis. He had made the pages of one of Argentina's most important literary magazines, and this gave him name recognition. Over the next 30 years, his writings would make the pages of this and other magazines in Buenos Aires, Argentina, Spain, and beyond.

A NEW LITERARY MENTOR

Not long after he returned with his family to Argentina, Borges became friends with one of his father's old schoolmates from law school, Macedonio Fernandez. Borges would write years later of the importance of Fernandez to himself and his writing career:

> Perhaps the major event of my return was Macedonio Fernandez. Of all the people I have met in my life—and I have met some quite remarkable men—no one has ever made so deep and so lasting an impression on me as Macedonio. A tiny figure in a black bowler hat, he was waiting for us on

> the Darsena Norte when we landed, and I came to inherit his friendship with my father.[53]

Fernandez was, indeed, a unique person in the life of Jorge Luis. He was a bohemian, "a frail, grey man with the kind of ash-colored hair and moustache that made him look like Mark Twain."[54] He was an eccentric, who did not undress when he went to bed, and he wrapped a towel around his head when he slept to keep drafts from giving him a toothache. He was a wanderer, an intellectual, and an anarchist, known for moving from one boarding house to the next and leaving behind the writings he had produced under each roof. He was unlike

WALKS WITH "MY MOST INTIMATE FRIEND"

As a young, aspiring writer, Jorge Borges commonly relied on close associates who could serve as mentors to him, or at least engage him regularly in stimulating dialogues. One such confidant and conversationalist was the poet Carlos Mastronardi. Borges would refer to him as "my most intimate friend."*

Mastronardi came from humble Argentine roots, a provincial young man who often wrote about the places he grew up, a "childhood of open skies and empty streets." The two men met in a bookstore. Mastronardi was bookish and wore glasses, and he loved to stay up until all hours of the night. He loved to lead the bohemian life, with his day starting when the Sun went down. He was a very deliberate writer and labored over his verses for hours.**

For several years during the late 1920s, the two spent many evenings walking through the seedier neighborhoods of Buenos Aires. Here, they both found inspiration for their poetry. These late afternoon and evening strolls through these suburbs sometimes resulted in personal experiences that made for stories worth telling later. In one set of poems, which he wrote decades after the actual events, Carlos remembered those wanderings with Borges.

Borges's previous mentor, Cansinos-Assens. For one thing, Fernandez was not as consistently brilliant a conversationalist, although he did host a group of literati on Saturday nights in the manner of Cansinos. It was during those sessions and in private talks with Jorge Luis that Fernandez left a strong mark on the young Argentine poet. He changed Jorge's perspective on the world, a major accomplishment for any mentor. Jorge described Fernandez's impact years later: "Before Macedonio, I had always been a credulous reader. His chief gift to me was to make me read skeptically."[55]

Macedonio was not an accomplished writer, in part because he rarely finished anything. When he struck up his

On one occasion, Jorge and Carlos were passing late one night through a slum neighborhood and became lost, finding themselves arriving at a local swamp. A policeman approached and told them to be careful because the neighborhood was a den of thieves and ruffians. The two friends quickly made up a story, telling the officer they were journalists on the trail of a news scoop. Whether he bought their story or not, he remained with them and took them back to a better-lit street.

As this pair of meandering poets searched such neighborhoods for inspiration for their poetry, they realized that they were walking along streets that for those who lived in such places, constituted little more than life in a slum. On one such occasion, in 1927, Borges and Mastronardi were making their way through the barrio of Saavedra, home to numberless tin shacks. Jorge Luis noted the poverty and hopelessness of the neighborhood, saying, "If we lived here we'd turn to bombs. No other way out!"***

* **Jason Wilson, *Jorge Luis Borges* (London: Reaktion Books, 2006), 62.**

** **Ibid.**

*** **Ibid., 63.**

relationship with young Borges, he had been writing manuscripts as early as 1896. Yet he was terribly unorganized and was always losing his papers. It would be Jorge Luis who would help him keep his literary papers together in one place, not left under the bed of the previous boarding house. They started a new magazine called *Proa (The Prow)*. It would be short lived, however. The magazine published only three issues between August 1922 and July 1923. Each was only six pages long. Jorge and Macedonio were the central figures of the literary effort, but they included other writers and poets. Sister Norah provided woodcut illustrations as she had done back in Spain for the ultraists.

Against the backdrop of these literary endeavors by himself, Macedonio, and the gang of ultraists, Jorge Luis had found someone else who dramatically influenced his life. It appears he had fallen in love with a 16-year-old girl named Concepción Guerrero. She lived in a Buenos Aires neighborhood located across town. She came from a poor family. The two had met, possibly, during the early months of 1922 at an address in the Belgrano quarter north of Palermo where Borges and his ultraists held many of their meetings. By mid-1922, he was infatuated with this younger beauty whose hair and dark eyes mesmerized him. They even became engaged, and, at times, the two seemed inseparable. From the beginning, the pairing was less than ideal. The two never advanced in their physical relationship beyond kissing, and Borges's mother, Leonor, did not approve of Concepción. Jorge Luis and Concepción would never marry.

A DRIVEN POET

Perhaps the most important result of their courtship was that during those months Jorge Luis was writing much poetry, driven to put his feelings into words. This writing led to the publication of his first collection of his early poems (eventually, there would be three such volumes), a work titled *Fervor de Buenos Aires (Adoration of Buenos Aires)*. The "Buenos Aires" of the title was a metaphor for his 16-year-old Concepción. It was as boyish a work as his immature love was for his young female companion. As he described the collection later:

> I wrote these poems in 1921 and 1922, and the volume came out early in 1923. . . . I had bargained for sixty-four pages, but the manuscript ran too long and at the last minute five poems had to be left out—mercifully. I can't remember a single thing about them. . . . No proofreading was done, no table of content was provided, and the pages were unnumbered. My sister made a woodcut for the cover, and three hundred copies were printed.[56]

Jorge Luis's father paid for the printing at a peso a copy. To help Borges with his first published book, *Nosotros* editor Bianchi agreed to distribute 50 copies through his office. Curiously, he did not hand them out directly to people. Instead, he discretely placed them in the overcoat pockets of important literary people who passed through his doors. This quiet technique further introduced Borges to those who had their fingers on the pulse of Argentine literature. They were introduced to his book and to its author, and "Borge's reputation grew on the back of *Fervor* not as an Ultraist, but as a Buenos Aires poet-dreamer."[57] As for the poems in the book, many focused on the dark, abused corners of Buenos Aires, as well as about Jorge's fiancée, Concepción. He wrote about the simple streets of the quiet, half-awake suburbs where one could walk and find solitude. *Fervor* would become and remain one of Borges's most famous works.

A CHANGE OF LOCATION

Just as Jorge Luis's name was beginning to be known in the literary circles of Buenos Aires and beyond, he left the city with his family in 1923 to accompany his father on a trip to Europe for another eye surgery. They stayed in Geneva until late spring and then moved on to Spain. The days spent in Spain had an

(*continues on page 50*)

BEING HISPANIC

REDISCOVERING THE ROOTS OF HISPANIC LITERATURE

Today, Jorge Luis Borges, touted by his fellow countrymen as the greatest writer their nation has ever produced, lies in a grave thousands of miles from his homeland of Argentina. He is removed not only by distance but by his literary legacy. That he chose to be buried in Switzerland, where his family lived through the twilight years of World War I, rather than in his homeland, speaks to his modern-day admirers. Borges, throughout his life, did not simply see himself as an Argentine writer or even, in a slightly broader context, a Hispanic writer. Instead, he was a writer, one whose words found willing readers everywhere.

Yet all this is not to suggest that Jorge Luis Borges is not, by definition on some level, a Hispanic writer, or that his literary output did not reflect the same. To deny that basic birthright is to deny that his being Hispanic had any impact on his writing at all. Instead, Borges should be seen as a literary bridge for Latin-American literature. He had a deep understanding of what it meant to have descended from heroic Spanish blood, and he spent his life reading and explaining the works of earlier Spanish writers, such as Cervantes, Quevedo, and San Juan de la Cruz. That he continued to write in Spanish helped to keep him connected to the written words of these earlier Hispanic writers. He was then able to deliver the works of those earlier Spaniards to those Latin writers of the modern, twentieth-century Hispanic literature.

In many ways, prior to the arrival of Borges on the literary scene, Spanish literature had fallen by the wayside. It had devolved into "a literature which until [the 20th century] looked as though it were worn out."* Yet he did more than simply revive Spanish writing. He managed to go back in time and discover the roots of Hispanic writing and even culture, by tapping "the Jewish and Arab traditions in Hispanic literary culture."** Through such approaches and historic reaching, Jorge Luis Borges was able to invent a new Hispanic writing.

This did not come about because he lived his life unconditionally in love with all things Spanish. Indeed, he did not. Throughout much of his life, he seemed to have a greater appreciation for the literature and culture of Great Britain, rather than the land of much of his ethnic heritage. Perhaps as an Argentine, he had a healthy skepticism of Spaniards, even referring to them as "slick and superficial."*** Spaniards were a constant target for Borges and his quick wit. He was as prone to mock them as he was to project them onto the pages of his literary works as emblematic of those ideals he considered worthwhile. He certainly did not reject the Hispanic world of his heritage or of his adulthood.

It must be remembered that Borges often returned to the streets of Buenos Aires and its suburbs for constant inspiration. Its dark, sketchy back streets are found in his poetry. The inhabitants of these fringe worlds would become fodder for his novels. He wrote numerous essays about life in these streets of his native land. These were quintessential Hispanic subjects, Hispanic topics, and Hispanic hemispheres that Borges never abandoned, even as he was constantly introduced to other cultures, other peoples, and other hemispheres. He was Hispanic, it was in his blood, and he found a place for it all in his writings.

One may put distance between himself and his blood heritage, but he will never fully outrun it. Borges chose, instead, to be selective in his being Hispanic. Those aspects of such a personal identity that he did not admire, he mocked or cast aside. Yet there were other influences of his Hispanic heritage—his family history, his love of Spanish literature, the Spanish language, and even Spain itself—that would help mold Jorge Luis Borges into the man he would become and the writer that people around the world would admire and read.

* James Woodall, *Borges, A Life* (New York: BasicBooks, 1996), 259.

** Ibid.

*** Ibid., 98.

(*continued from page 47*)

important result for Borges's sister, Norah. When they had lived there earlier, she had met Guillermo de Torre, another ultraist writer, and had a relationship with him. Once again, they had the opportunity to reconnect. (Five years later, the two would marry.) Borges even met up with his old mentor, Cansinos-Assens. Their visit overlapped the arrival of *Fervor* in Spain where it was favorably reviewed in an important Spanish literary journal, further advancing Borges's reputation as a poet. On the downside, Jorge Luis found that the ultraist movement had practically fizzled out in Spain, causing him to long to return to Argentina. It was there that his most important reputation was already firming up.

When the family returned to Argentina in spring 1924, Borges knew his destiny as a writer would be made there. Even more specifically, he was beginning to understand that it was his purpose as a poet and essayist to explain to the outside world just exactly what Argentina *was.* Within just a few years, his literary allegiance to Argentina would lead him to practically reject ultraism and cling to another literary approach he called "*criollismo.*" Through this new approach, he rejected the significance of his Spanish heritage and emphasized his native Argentine roots, his ethnic "creole" roots.

To an Argentine, the term "creole" referred to "white Spaniards who lived in the Spanish colony and had been born on the River Plate; in other words, the original inhabitants of a Buenos Aires that was then a smugglers' backwater."[58] Borges worked hard to affect this identity for himself (it helped that he had spent seven years in Spain) by studying traditional Argentine phrases. This meant dropping the final 'd' from words and altering 'g' sounds to 'j' and 'y' sounds to 'i.' To round out his transformation, he insisted he be called Jorge rather than Georgie, the nickname that had dogged him since infancy. He later thought he might have overdone it all: "I made the mistake of trying to be more Argentine than the Argentines."[59]

The pampa is the rugged plains found around Buenos Aires and other provinces in Argentina as well as other parts of South America, including Uruguay and Brazil. To Borges, this fertile landscape represented part of his heritage, and he knew that his career as a writer would be found in his Argentine homeland.

Despite what might have been some excesses, however, he had found his place and largely found his voice. His future lay in the city and in the rural regions of the rugged Argentine landscape, the pampa. Once he stepped foot back on Argentine soil, he wasted no time writing about his homeland, or at least the parts of it that appealed to him the most. He became intrigued with the seedier neighborhoods of Buenos Aires. He tried to identify with the residents of these disreputable suburbs by learning to dance the tango and hanging out with street toughs, hustlers, and hoodlums. (In the meantime, Borges and Concepción broke off their relationship, and Borges would never mention her in his writings again.)

SUCCESS AND DISAPPOINTMENT

Borges was soon extremely busy, contributing to various magazines and journals. He was a regular writer for *Martín Fierro*, a well-established, antiestablishment literary journal. At the time, two literary groups were adding their voices to such magazines, the Boedo and Florida Groups. The Boedo Group was driven by its working-class, bourgeoisie writers who wrote rough, realistic pieces. The Florida Group writers were heavily influenced by European styles and the avant-garde. Sometimes Borges fit in either and both groups, but he did not place much importance on allegiance to one or the other.

Also, in 1924, he worked on reestablishing *Proa* magazine. He was aided by a new group of influential, mentoring writers that included poets Ricardo Guiraldes and Alfredo Brandan Caraffa and novelist Pablo Rojas Paz. Guiraldes was especially influential. These associations continued Borges's habit during these formative years of relying on mentors to guide his writing. The new *Proa* stayed in print for two years, during which Borges published a second book of poetry titled *Luna de enfrente (Moon Across the Way)*. He also published a pair of essay collections, *Inquisiciones (Inquisitions)* and *El tamaño de mi esperanza (The Size of My Hope)*. The latter focused on Jorge's growing interest in all things Jewish, including literature, religion, culture, and traditional folklore. At the end of *Proa*'s publication run, Jorge Luis found yet another mentor, writer Alfonso Reyes, from Mexico. They met in Buenos Aires where Reyes had served as an ambassador. Reyes emphasized to Borges the importance of keeping his writing simple and direct. By this time, Jorge was gaining a greater level of maturity in his writing, and it caused him to become embarrassed about his earlier compositions. He now thought those were the ramblings of an emotional and inexperienced youth.

Having ended his relationship with the teenaged Concepción, he struck up a strong friendship with 17-year-old Elsa Astete Millan, to whom he was introduced by a friend. Shortly after meeting her, he was interested in marriage, although he soon discovered a complication. Elsa did not return his attentions, and when he called her house, Elsa's mother would usually answer the phone. When Borges asked why Elsa never came to the phone, her mother explained, "Georgie, I'm sorry, Elsa is engaged to be married to someone else."[60] This brought an immediate end to his friendship with the teenaged girl. Seventeen years would pass before he even saw her again. Yet they would one day, indeed, marry each other.

While relationships with women, especially romantic relationships, were difficult, awkward, and even disastrous for Borges, he had much better results with his literary relationships. Two additional artistic friends came into Jorge Luis's circle by the late 1920s. One was a half-Italian, half-Lithuanian abstract artist named Alejandro Schulz Solari, who went by the foreshortened name, Xul Solar. The other was the writer Carlos Mastronardi. Xul Solar befriended Borges through their mutual membership in the *Martín Fierro* group. (He also exhibited his art alongside Norah Borges in 1926.) The two men had lengthy conversations on everything from mathematics to astrology to the symbolism of the Jewish kabbalah. (The kabbalah is a system of Jewish mysticism that dates back to medieval times.) Mastronardi, who was two years younger than Borges and shared his love of British writer G.K. Chesterton and detective stories, accompanied Borges on his long nighttime walks through the back streets of Buenos Aires. Jorge Luis would refer to him as "an inseparable friend of the night."[61]

4

Writer in Transition

Another relationship would also change for Borges by the late 1920s. In 1928, Norah accepted a proposal of marriage from her longtime friend from Spain, Guillermo de Torre. The new couple moved to Spain following the wedding. This would bring about a separation for the brother and sister that would never be mended. Their childhood days of shared closeness would never be replicated. In fact, in their later years, Jorge and Norah's "relations became strained and unpleasant."[62]

POLITICS AND POETRY

For a while in 1928, Borges dabbled overtly in politics. That year, Hipólito Irigoyen, a member of Argentina's Radical Party, was trying to make a political comeback. The 77-year-old politician had served as the nation's president from 1916 to 1922. During the presidential election, Irigoyen campaigned on behalf of Argentina's economic independence and for social justice. Borges gave him his support by hosting a meeting at his house that included artists and poets who were his friends and colleagues. He encouraged them to rally behind Irigoyen. The former president was elected to another term. Borges did not remain closely tied to Argentine politics after Irigoyen's election, possibly because the reelected president failed to accomplish many of his political goals.

In 1929, Borges published a book of poems, *Cuaderno San Martín.* (The title was taken from a name of a type of notebook that was popular at that time in Buenos Aires.) This was a short work, consisting of only 11 poems. It included two poems about Buenos Aires's most important cemeteries and one about his grandfather, who had died when Jorge Luis was only five years old. A book of essays, *El Idioma de los argentinos (The Language of the Argentines),* came next and was soon followed by a surprise affirmation of Borges's writing and his contribution to the literature of his city. He received the Second Municipal Prize of 3,000 pesos. The record is not clear whether he won the honor for *El Idioma de los argentinos* or *Cuaderno San Martín,* but Borges excitedly went out and purchased a used copy of the *Encyclopaedia Britannica,* 11th edition, with the prize money. This encyclopedia became one of his constant sources of reference and would remain so for the rest of his life. (From his childhood, Jorge Luis Borges had a fascination with encyclopedias, and he referred to them frequently when writing.)

Borges had money left over following this important purchase, and he intended to make good use of it. He was still living in his father's household, along with his mother, father, and grandmother Fanny Haslam. The family had moved after Norah's marriage, downsizing from the house on avenida Quintana to the corner of avenidas Las Hera and Pueyrredon, "a fifth-floor flat with seven balconies."[63] In this new residence, and using what money he had left from his literary prize, Jorge was able to reduce his dependence on making money through writing poetry and essays for magazines. He was now able to focus for a lengthy period of time on a longer project, "an extended piece of prose on a purely Argentine theme, a biography perhaps."[64] After taking suggestions from his parents, he chose not to pick one of Argentina's great writers of the nineteenth century but rather on his poet-friend, Evaristo Carriego.

In reality, much of the book he produced was about the city of Buenos Aires, and the work did not sell particularly well. Most of its readers were his friends. It would prove to be a "strange, flawed, and today virtually unreadable tome, hastily researched, and cobbled together."[65] In the bigger picture, however, *Evaristo Carriego* did prove to be an important work. It would become the only book Borges produced during this period that he allowed to be printed in later years. Borges rejected much of what he produced during the 1920s, describing that poetry as "youthful and overly drenched in local color."[66] As a result, Borges would come to think of *The Size of My Hope, The Language of the Argentines,* and *Inquisitions* as unworthy of his talent. He disallowed them to be reprinted, and "whenever he noticed the books on friends' shelves, he would ask for permission to destroy their copies."[67]

A NEW AND DIFFERENT DECADE

Evaristo Carriego marked the end of a decade for Jorge Luis on a sour note. The new decade would deliver new difficulties, losses, and failure for Borges, yet there were also new influences, companions, and mentors. Throughout the 1930s, three individuals had great impact on the Argentinian writer but none more than a woman, Victoria Ocampo, nearly a decade older than Borges. He first met her in 1925 during the publication of *Proa.* She was a tall, handsome, free-thinking woman of wealth who descended from French aristocracy and one of the oldest families in Argentina. If Borges was shy, she was extremely outgoing. She would later describe Jorge Luis as "a young man with a certain shyness apparent

Victoria Ocampo (1890–1979), born in Buenos Aires, was once described by Borges as "the most Argentine woman." Ocampo was the publisher of *Sur*, a magazine that featured many of the finest literary voices of the time, including Borges. Ocampo was also a writer and critic.

in the way he walked, in his voice, in his handshake, and his eyes."[68] With Borges, she had found someone she could work to change, especially his attitudes concerning women.

Ocampo was a literary figure in her own right, launching a magazine for writers called *Sur (South)* in 1931. All the poets and essayists of the new generation wrote for the literary journal, including Aldous Huxley, Alfonso Reyes, André Gide, Virginia Woolfe, and Jorge Luis Borges. The magazine was a grand step above the usual literary rag for which Borges had previously written. (*Sur's* first issue was 199 pages in length, printed on expensive paper, and illustrated by the great Spanish artist Pablo Picasso.) Ocampo and the opportunities she afforded Borges through the pages of *Sur* were highly important to his reputation as a writer entering the 1930s. He abandoned ultraism and criollismo, as well as his drive to be purely Argentine. The magazine let him expand as a writer, and his reputation became less "American" and more international. He was bent on reinventing himself as a writer. To that end, he began to steer toward modernism and to embrace "metaphysics, philosophy, and the fantastical, and his style began to develop into something wholly original."[69]

Another important influence on Borges during the 1930s was Nestor Ibarra. He arrived in Buenos Aires from France during the mid-1920s to further his studies at the university's Faculty of Philosophy and Letters. He was already an admirer of Borges's poetry. The two met at a dinner party in 1928, and, according to Ibarra, they left together, as Borges "made me go fifteen kilometers [nine miles] in two hours."[70] The two would spend years together as friends and literary compatriots. They played word games with one another and made up new words such as *phanerogamic*, a term describing underdressed beachgoers. During the 1940s, Ibarra would make an important contribution to Borges's legacy, by translating Jorge's writings into French. This would open up yet another international door for his Argentine companion. Without Ibarra's efforts, Borges might have remained a writer who was read only in Spanish for a much longer period.

In spring 1932, Borges met the third of his important influences of that decade, at a party at Victoria Ocampo's house. His name was Adolfo Bioy Casares, and he was only 17 years old. Jorge would always refer to him as "Bioy." The young man was outgoing to the point of being precocious. At their first meeting, Borges quizzed him about his favorite writers of the twentieth century. When Casares answered Gabriel Miró, Azorin, and James Joyce, Borges was pleased. He informed Bioy that only in such figures could young writers find "enough literature to satisfy them."[71] The two were immediately fast friends.

Bioy was literary, an avid reader, gregarious, and wealthy. (His father's family owned an estate in Pardo, while his mother's family ran a dairy farm and "owned over a hundred milk bars in Buenos Aires."[72]) He was different than Borges in that he was charming, handsome, a sporty tennis player, and an accomplished ladies man. Yet the two remained friends for the remainder of Borges's life.

The new decade delivered new recognition for Borges. The publication of a new collection of essays, *Discusción*, included pieces on his literary tastes, as well as his interest in film. While he regularly wrote reviews of literary works, he was also writing reviews of the cinema. (His work as an editor and reviewer gave him cause to read an incredible number of books. From 1936 to 1939, he reviewed more than 200 books for one magazine alone, and he was reviewing books for other magazines at that time.) His film tastes were simple and included such genres as American Westerns and musicals, including *My Fair Lady* and *West Side Story*. He was a big fan of the works of British film director, Alfred Hitchcock. To Borges, film was becoming an important medium. "Cinema," he once said, "has answered, probably without meaning to, two eternal needs of the soul: melodrama and epic."[73]

Borges had become so recognized that, in 1933, one journal, *Megáfono*, published an entire issue exclusively featuring Borges's writing. Borges was even trying his hand at new literary forms. This led to his first short story, "Streetcorner Man," which centered on a knife fight. It was just the kind of scene

Borges could easily witness during nighttime walks through Buenos Aires's poor suburbs. It ran in a popular newspaper whose literary pages Borges edited. (Not certain of the reaction his story would receive, Borges used his great-great grandfather's name, Francisco Bustos, as a pen name.)

"HOAX FICTION"

Between 1933 and 1934, Borges published a half dozen pieces in *Critica* that would later be printed in a book titled *Historia universal de la infamia (A Universal History of Infamy).* The book also included "Streetcorner Man." Jorge Luis later gave the book significant credit: "The real beginning of my career as a story writer starts with the series of sketches entitled *Historia universal de la infamia.*"[74] The work revealed an experimental Borges, for he used his talent to create fictional biographies of actual figures, including American Western gunslinger Billy the Kid. Blending fact with fiction, Borges was setting out on yet another new course for his writing. He was about to plunge into the world of surrealism and "hoax fiction."

His first actual hoax fiction work was a story that he wrote as a book review of a novel that did not actually exist. The piece, "The Approach to al-Mu'tasim," was so well written that his friend Bioy believed the novel Borges was reviewing actually existed. Many literary critics consider this work to be the first real "Borgesian" story. The work appeared in his next published essay collection, *Historia de al eternidad (History of Eternity).* The collection was not popular, because, according to Borges, only 37 copies were sold. In an interview years later, Borges apologized to the 37 people who had bought the book.

Even as some of Borges's books were not selling well, his reputation as a writer was gaining with each passing year during the 1930s. All was not well with Borges, however, especially in his private life. His nearly constant struggle was with depression, and it dogged him emotionally. His friend Bioy described Borges as a man who projected outer happiness but

Adolfo Bioy Casares (1914–1999) was a celebrated Argentine fiction writer and Borges's longtime friend and collaborator. In addition to producing numerous stories together, the pair also wrote several screenplays.

suffered from "a base of sadness, on the inside."[75] Some critics even believe he may have been suicidal during this period. The causes of his dark thoughts probably included failures in his personal life and the political climate in Argentina.

A NEW LITERARY DECADE

The 1930s was the decade of a worldwide depression that hit all industrial nations from the Americas to Asia hard.

The worst effects did not land as heavily on Argentina, but it caused a general anxiousness in the country that led to political instability. In 1930, President Irigoyen, whom Borges had campaigned for and later rejected, was overthrown by a rightist government that brought conservative leader José Uriburu to office. President Uriburu was then himself ousted the following year by General Augustin Justo. For the next seven years, Justo ruled militarily through election rigging and the elimination of political opponents until President Roberto Ortiz came to power in 1938. By then, full-scale war had broken out across Europe with the rise of the dictatorships of Germany's Adolf Hitler and Italy's Benito Mussolini. Even

BORGES AND HIS FIRST STORY, "STREETCORNER MAN"

By the early 1930s, Jorge Luis Borges was constantly publishing and editing with regularity and making his mark on the literary tastes of his day. He was experimenting with his writing and developing new ways of formulating ideas on the printed page. In 1933, he published his first short story, "Streetcorner Man," an extremely important work.

"Streetcorner Man" was essentially a gangster piece that Borges claimed he wrote over a six-year period from 1927 to 1933. He later recalled how he "[slaved] over every sentence, getting the voice exact."* The work focused on the seedy, backstreet activities of the thugs and tough guys who roamed the alley ways of Palermo. Borges always had a great admiration for the rough characters he witnessed during his walks through the shady regions around Buenos Aires. The contrast between writers such as himself and the streetwise ruffians he came to know was important to him. He thought of himself and other middle-class citizens as little more than cowards, but he thought of these underworld figures as real men who proved their manhood

Spain would experience a civil war by 1936 that would bring the fascist Generalissimo Francisco Franco to power. The late 1930s found Argentina neutral regarding the ever-expanding World War II, but in the grip of a harsh nationalism that was prepared to surrender democracy completely.

Borges spoke out even as his native country remained neutral. He was afraid that fascism would take over his homeland, a fear that would soon become realized. He also spoke out against anti-Semitism, one of Nazi Germany's strongest themes. Borges did not side with the Argentine nationalist movement but chose instead to support the European powers that were fighting for democracy. On a literary level, Borges, most of his compatriots, and the pages of *Sur* rallied behind

through wars and duels. Borges always envied these "men of action," whom he considered the embodiment of machismo.

"Streetcorner Man" is a story set in a dance hall and brothel in the northern part of Buenos Aires. The action involves a street type who enters the establishment and challenges another man to a knife duel. The challenged thug refuses to fight and even throws down his knife, as Borges sees it, like a coward. The challenger leaves the dance hall with the second man's girl. Shortly, she returns to the room, announcing that the knife-wielding challenger has been stabbed to death.

Borges later thought the story to be a failure, considering the work to be "bogus, stagy and mannered." Yet he chose to write another version of the street encounter from the viewpoint of the story's "coward," a work titled "The Story from Rosendo Juarez."**

* Jason Wilson, *Jorge Luis Borges* (London: Reaktion Books, 2006), 92.

** Ibid.

the Allies, including France and Great Britain, and opposed German and Italian fascism. This political turmoil caused depression in Borges.

He was also influenced darkly by his private, personal worlds. His vision was becoming a problem. He had, indeed, inherited his family's eye frailties, which led to his first eye operation, for cataracts, in 1927. Borges also struggled with insomnia, a condition with which he suffered for years. In a poem he published during the mid-1930s, titled "Insomnia," he referred to his condition as an "appalling wakefulness."[76]

Yet as much as his eye problems plagued him by the 1930s, Borges was also struggling with his love life, or the lack of one. He was by now a heavyset man in his mid-thirties with eye trouble. He had never gained a true confidence with women. Ironically, many of those females with whom he rubbed shoulders professionally were "usually rich, sophisticated, and beautiful, a contrast to Borges who was poor and shy."[77] He could not find intimacy. He was increasingly drawn toward his mother, who was still taking care of many of his personal needs. At home, things were not well either. Still living under his father's roof, he experienced the death of his 93-year-old grandmother Fanny in 1935. Thirty five years later, Borges would commemorate her death in a poem titled "Variación," in which he referred to her as having said just before death: "Let me die in peace."[78] His father too was in poor health, nearly blind, "a sad, unfulfilled figure, who sat for hours in silence, staring into nothingness."[79] His father, Jorge, suffered from a heart condition as well. Nearly incapacitated, he was almost constantly cared for by his wife, Leonor. All this old age, declining health, and deceased loved ones were further catalysts for Borges's depression.

FIRST EMPLOYMENT

Although Borges was a busy writer during the 1930s, he was not making much money. He had always avoided taking a regular job for the sake of his literary career but had that really proven to be worth it in the end? He described himself as "long past the age when I should have begun contributing to our household upkeep."[80] In 1937, he took his first real job, one arranged through the influences of Bioy's family. It seemed an appropriate work for a somewhat successful writer. It was a job at a municipal library located in the working-class neighborhood of Almagro Sur on Carlos Calvo 4319, across town from Borges's home. To get there, Borges had to take a long streetcar ride and then walk 10 blocks.

The job did not pay well, starting out at 210 pesos monthly and later increased to 240 pesos, the modern-day equivalent of about $80. The library, however, would be a part of Borges's life for nearly 10 years, from mid-1937 to August 1946. They would be, as Jorge Luis described them, "nine years of solid unhappiness."[81] His title was First Assistant, and his duties included classifying and cataloguing the library's book collection. The library was overstaffed with more than 50 workers, three times the number actually needed. These were government jobs, and one of the first criticisms leveled against Borges came from his fellow workers who wanted him to slow down in his work: "You'll put us out of our jobs."[82] It also seemed that no one working at the library was interested in literature. (One clueless employee once marveled that Borges and an author he discovered in an encyclopedia had the same name and birth date!) The other workers did not even realize at first that their new colleague was an author. The job became and remained a misery to Borges.

The job, however, did give him opportunity to continue his literary work. Once he had finished the library tasks for that day, he would wander off to a corner of the library basement and write, as well as read and translate others' works. He would be the first to put the words of such authors as Virginia Woolf and William Faulkner into Spanish. Borges naturally took advantage of his daily train rides, which he passed reading works by Bernard Shaw, Franz Kafka, Edward Gibbon, and Dante. Using an Italian/English version of

Dante's epic poem, *The Divine Comedy*, Borges was able to teach himself Italian.

A PAIR OF TRAGEDIES

The following year brought two tragedies into the life of Jorge Luis Borges. The first came just months after Borges started his library job. His father died on February 24, delivering a heavy loss to his son. During the last three years of his life, his vision had improved following an operation in 1935, but he had remained a disappointed man. His death had been quickened by his refusal to eat or take his medications. Before his father's passing, Borges made a promise to him that he, at his father's request, would rewrite the only novel the senior Jorge had ever written. It would prove to be an unkept promise. Borges never took up his father's literary endeavor, and, in later years, he would regret having made the promise.

Toward the end of the year, another tragedy occurred. On Christmas Eve, Borges had a freak accident. While running up a flight of stairs in an apartment building, he bumped into a freshly painted window that had been left open inward over the staircase. In his rush, and probably due to his poor eyesight, he failed to see it. In a later work, he described the mishap nonchalantly: "I felt something brush my scalp."[83] It was more than just a simple scrape to the head, however. The glass had shattered, and pieces were embedded in his head. His mother treated the wound, but it became badly infected, producing a high fever and hallucinations. By the time he went to a hospital, he was completely unable to speak. For the next month, his survival was touch and go.

The incident, however, did have another effect on Borges. During his weeks in the hospital, he gave much thought to his life and began to have serious doubts about his mental capacities. He even thought he might be going insane. Through this valley, Borges came to some serious revelations, as are described by Borges biographer, James Woodall:

His mother read to him from C.S. Lewis's *Out of the Silent Planet.* He cried, and when she asked him why, he replied "because I understand." And he also understood something to do with what he should do next, something to do with his next step as a writer. He was full of doubts about that step, but knew he should, somehow, prepare for the "final revelation." He should write a story. Amidst such circumstantial confusion, and yet with so simple a formula, a mid-century revolution in the art of fiction was about to begin.[84]

5

Poetry and Power

One of the reasons why Borges cried in his hospital bed was his fear that his accident might have somehow taken away his creative abilities. It may have been a strange dread, but he could not have been further from the truth. In fact, he emerged from his dramatic ordeal with a renewed sense of direction and commitment. He described his recommitment to his writing more clearly during a 1964 interview:

> If I begin to write, if I dare to write an article on some book or another and I cannot do it, I'm finished, I don't exist any more. To make this discovery a little less dreadful, I'm going to try and do something I've never done. If I don't succeed, it'll be less dreadful for me. That at least will prepare me for accepting a non-literary destiny. Therefore I shall do something I've never done before: I shall write a story.[85]

"FICTIVE REALITY"

It was through this realization that Borges began revamping his fiction and took up short story writing. Two stories immediately reset the pathway of his career. They were published about a year apart in *Sur* and were titled, "Pierre Menard, Author of the *Quixote*" and "Tlon, Uqbar, Orbis Tertius." The first was a hoax story wrapped in the guise of a literary criticism. The second was even more innovative. It concerned the discovery of a fictional country as if it really existed. It gave Borges an opportunity to declare his fears concerning the developing war in Europe and the threat of fascism, which he believed was going to take over Argentina's politics. These works mark the beginning of Borges's experiments with "fictive reality." They were strange stories that confused their readers and included characters who were real people, such as Borges himself. These were creatively different approaches to writing fiction. They were Borges's *ficciones,* which combined "complex critiques of realism [while] posing questions of identity."[86]

After the accident, life more or less continued as before with a few significant changes. His sister returned to Argentina from Paris with her new husband, Guillermo de Torre. For a time, they lived with Borges and Leonor, but, in early 1939, Jorge Luis and his mother moved to a house at calle Anchorena 1672, a large home with an inner courtyard and a modest garden. Borges's library work continued, and he produced new stories, which would be published in book form in 1941 under the title *El jardin de senderos que se bifurcan (The Garden of Forking Paths).* This collection redefined Borges's approach to fiction. It ignored traditional formats and boundaries while functioning on several complex levels of narration. A seemingly simple detective story became a philosophical maze. There was an allegory about his library work, titled "The Library of Babel." He was using not only literary techniques in his new story style, but he also employed his "growing fascination with metaphysics, ancient Gnostics, and mathematical notions."[87] To his readers, the stories were odd and confusing. To his mother, they played on her fears that her son might actually be going mad.

Perhaps no one really understood these works or got the joke as well as Borges's friend Bioy. Both understood the value of writing to spoof, parody, or otherwise tweak the noses of critics and readers alike. In 1942, they even published several detective stories together. Their intent was to spoof the genre while complicating their pages with inside jokes and mixed-up story lines. To these two writers, the game had become to laugh at their readers and themselves. As Borges later described their efforts, "So we have created between us a kind of third person; we have somehow begotten a third person that is quite unlike us."[88]

FASCISM AND THE RISE OF PERÓN

Against these significant changes in the literary art of Jorge Luis Borges during the late 1930s and early 1940s, great political change was coming to Argentina. Although Borges had never been an overtly political figure, these events troubled him. He had watched as the Allies and Axis powers had fought across Europe, Africa, and the Mediterranean during World War II, and he was extremely joyful when the Allies liberated Paris from German occupation in late summer 1944. Events at home, however, were now occupying his attention. Political instability had continued into the new decade, leading to the ouster of President Castillo by the army, led by General Pedro Ramirez. Before he was removed in 1944, the general agreed to cut off diplomatic ties with Nazi Germany. Another general soon took his place, and the army squashed all political parties.

Out of this political infighting and military power-playing rose Colonel Juan Domingo Perón, who became Argentina's vice president. Perón soon stood out from his military-political associates by gaining support from Argentines in this

Juan Domingo Perón (1895–1974) was an Argentine general who was elected three times as president of Argentina. Although many Argentines believed Perón was bringing positive change to the nation, Borges thought he was a dictator and publicly criticized the president. Perón is shown here with his wife, Eva, in 1950.

divisive atmosphere. He spoke out favorably concerning workers' rights and economic independence for his country. He was an anti-imperialist who was also staunchly anti-British. (To many Argentines, the British epitomized the heart and soul of imperialism.) Popular opinion in Argentina ran closely in sync with Perón's public statements, and he projected a certain charisma that appealed to the populace. He had a large smile, a voice that played well on the radio, and a blond mistress, Eva Duarte, an actress who also projected herself into the hearts and minds of the people of Argentina. (They would marry on October 22, 1945.) Borges hated Perón, thinking that the vice president was hungry for power and was a fascist. As Perón gained increasing political power, Jorge Luis would lament how, from his perspective, "a great number of Argentines are becoming Nazis without being aware of it."[89]

A PROPOSAL OF MARRIAGE

During these days of political unrest in Argentina, Borges was falling in love with a woman, Estela Canto. They met just prior to the liberation of Paris in August 1944. When Borges referred to the freeing of the French capital as causing himself "physical happiness," he may also have felt the same for this 28-year-old woman from Uruguay, whose landholding roots had fallen on hard times. Canto was "dark, slim, with large brown, knowing eyes . . . street-wise and politically motivated—leftwards."[90] (She hated Perón as much as Borges.) She was intelligent, financially independent, politically savvy, and a lover of literature. She even accompanied Borges on his ramblings throughout the city, speaking with him in English. When she told Jorge Luis that her favorite author was Bernard Shaw, he told her he had never met another woman who even liked Shaw. He was smitten.

Estela seemed to like him, somewhat. She would write, "Everything Borges said had a magical quality. . . . They were magical because they suggested the man he really was, the man hidden behind the Georgie whom we knew, a man who, in his shyness, was struggling to emerge, to be recognized."[91] They soon became the equivalent of boy- and girlfriend, talking about literature, taking their walks, going to the movies, and sharing candlelit dinners. (Borges apparently always ate the same thing: rice soup, steak, cheese, and quince jam.) They kissed, but this was never the highlight of an evening spent together. Estela referred to Borges's kisses as "awkward, brusque, always ill-timed."[92]

After eight or nine months of "dating," Borges proposed marriage to her. It happened after dinner at the Hotel Las Delicias in Adrogue. They had walked to the nearest train station, as he quoted Dante and held tightly to her arm. At the station, he wanted to turn back and walk some more. Finally, they stopped on the street, each standing at the opposite end of a cement bench. Through the darkness, he surprised her with the question. He had miscalculated, however. Estela had strong feelings for him, but she did not love him enough to marry him. She was not actually sexually attracted to the man who was nearly 20 years older than herself. (Their physical relationship had never advanced past the kissing stage. Borges always struggled with powerful sexual hang-ups, making a sexual relationship almost unthinkable. The idea of sex with a woman actually petrified him.) She turned down his marriage proposal.

Their relationship did not end, however. They continued to see one another, but their relationship became more complicated and strained with time. Estela knew that Borges's mother did not approve of her, and Estela did not care for Leonor. It seemed odd to this young woman that a man of Borges's age would still be relying so significantly on his mother's support. There were arguments between Leonor, Borges, and Estela. Borges became so depressed about it that he may have considered suicide. Then, Argentine politics and Borges's relationship with Estela crossed paths. As the political climate worsened, Estela decided to leave Buenos Aires. Soon, Jorge Luis and Estela saw less of one another until their relationship faded. By the end of November 1945, she left for Uruguay, where she soon had a love affair with an Englishman. She would later recall, "I spent some of the most beautiful months of my entire life with him. I totally forgot about Georgie, whom in a way I treated badly."[93]

PERÓN IN POWER

New twists were about to enter the life of Jorge Luis Borges, starting with the election of Juan Perón as president in February 1946. Borges had never hidden his contempt and had written about the general on several occasions. It came as no surprise to Borges that almost immediately after the election, he lost his library position. (Someone in the Perón government tried to humiliate Borges by "promoting" him from the library to inspector of poultry and rabbits.) Life was collapsing all around him. The 47-year-old Jorge Luis was no longer employed after nine miserable years. He had other work, however, because he had become the editor of a new literary magazine, *Anales de Buenos Aries,* and his literary contributions to *Sur* had never ended. Yet he had little opportunity to make any real money. He was depressed by his new realities. He was middle-aged, essentially unemployed, on the rebound from a lost love, and politically on the wrong side of the fence. Borges was experiencing a midlife crisis.

Although never an admirer of the Father of Psychiatry, Sigmund Freud, Borges started twice-weekly sessions with another Jewish psychiatrist, Dr. Miguel Kohan-Miller, who was a fan of Borges's writings. Little is known concerning the sessions between Borges and Kohan-Miller. It seems likely that the subject of Jorge Luis's sexual hang-ups and general fears of intimacy with a woman were discussed at length. (Estela was actually asked to attend a session and talk with the doctor.) Perhaps Borges discussed his mother. Whatever happened during his therapy, two results appear clear. Borges would, finally, overcome some of his dread of sexual relations, and his emotions were lifted enough to spur him onto greater levels of literary production and creativity.

Over the next year, he was writing constantly. (He and Leonor moved again, this time to a flat near the main business district of Buenos Aires.) Then, new opportunities came along. He was asked to teach English literature at the Argentine Association for English Culture. He was also approached by the Free College for Higher Studies to deliver a series of lectures on American literature. At first his attempts to speak publicly were disasters, and his fears caused him to stammer. He finally overcame this additional insecurity, probably due to the work of Dr. Kohan-Miller. For the remainder of his life, lecturing remained commonplace for him. He spoke on a wide variety of topics, from the poet William Blake to Buddhism to Jewish religion to Spanish writers. To help prepare for such lectures, he memorized his entire presentation and practiced with an audience of one, his mother, Leonor.

There were new successes for the middle-aged Borges. In 1949, he published a collection of stories, *El Aleph.* The word referred to a kaleidoscope, a children's toy that Borges had discovered a few years earlier. The grouping of 13 stories included subjects ranging from "gauchos, death, time, contradictory universes, metaphysics, and conundrums."[94]

In 1950, Borges was elected to the presidency of the Sociedad Argentina de Escritores, or SADE (Argentine Society for Writers). Officially, the organization was literary in nature, but it was exceedingly political and highly anti-Perónist. State officials monitored the group's meetings, and Borges was a special target. As early as 1948, police were routinely following him on his long walks, and undercover officials would show up at his lectures. (That same year, in September, when officials had broken up a group of women engaged in an anti-Perón demonstration, they had arrested his mother and sister. Leonor, then 72 years old, was placed under house arrest for a month. Norah was jailed for as many weeks in the Buen Pastor prison for women, in a cell block for prostitutes.) In 1953,

Borges, shown here in 1943, kept busy during the 1940s, writing, teaching, and lecturing. Despite the unpleasant politics of the time, Jorge Luis collaborated with his friend Bioy early in the decade, and in 1949, he published the acclaimed *El Aleph,* a collection of short stories that presented his views on human experience.

President Perón shut down SADE altogether, even though Borges had only recently resigned as the society's president. This political harassment infuriated Borges. With Perón in power, Buenos Aires had become, in Borges's eyes, "an occupied city."[95]

Even as politics continued to present stumbling blocks in the career of Jorge Luis Borges, the early 1950s brought him great success. In fact, from 1951 to 1955, Borges experienced three significant publishing milestones that would represent some of the most important highlights of his entire life. The first was the 1951 publication of his book *La muerte y la brujula,* a recollected edition of nine stories taken from the pages of *Ficciones* and *El Aleph.* The book became Borges's first commercially successful publication. The book's publisher, Emece, would continue to print other books of Borges's over the next 30 years.

On the heels of this success, two works by the Argentine author were published for the first time in French: *Ficciones* and a new collection of only four stories titled *Labyrinths,* the latter published in 1953. Suddenly, Borges's books were reaching a new audience. For the remainder of his career, the French were great fans of Jorge Luis. This was an extremely significant advancement in Borges's ultimate literary legacy:

> For French intellectuals and readers of "serious literature", Borges was the Ultimate item of collectability: stark, nightmarishly rational, self-reflective, somehow French in manner but utterly foreign in subject matter. Over the next decade, indeed, before he began his globetrotting, Borge was to be more consistently admired in France than anywhere in the world—including Argentina. The path towards global Borges was dug by the nation that, in its post-war intellectual restlessness, seemed to be waiting for him.[96]

The third literary success for Borges during the Perón years was the publication of a collection of essays, *Otras inquisiciónes*

(Other Inquisitions), in 1952. It was similar to the collection he had published 20 years earlier, *Discusión.* The work included 39 essays written over a 15-year period, and most of them consisted of literary criticism. Many of them had been published in *La Nación* newspaper. Thematically, its sources were quite broad, including many of Borges's individualistic literature tastes, such as Spanish poets and the English classical writers Coleridge and Keats. Included were his favorites: Hawthorne, Whitman, Chesterton, H.G. Wells, Bernard Shaw, and Kafka. The collection was not based on a theme or a proposed direction for the reader to follow. Instead, it was a jumble of works that reflected Borges and his multiple interests, including those of philosophy, literary connections, personal inquisitiveness, and his own views of time.

FIGHTING FOR HIS EYESIGHT

Throughout his life, Jorge Luis Borges was constantly aware that he was losing his eyesight. Even from his early years, he fought the condition that would make reading and writing an increasing difficulty. His first cataract surgery was in 1927. By the mid-1950s, he had undergone eight such operations. Yet his sight continued to dim. How did Borges react to this loss that continued for decades? How did he cope and still remain a writer?

It was not easy. As a middle-aged man he wrote of how his condition sometimes swung from bad to worse: "There was a moment where I could only read the title page or the words on the spine, and then another when I could read nothing at all."* Colors escaped from his vision as well. He would remember yellow as the last color he could see, recalling it as "the most vivid of colors."** With such losses, he had no choice but to reorganize himself to remain productive. He began arranging his bookshelves so that the books he often consulted, such as dictionaries, would be easily available. He knew them by touch and was often seen turning to certain pages by memory rather than sight.

END FOR PERÓN, BEGINNING FOR POETRY

Such literary successes for Borges helped him to cope with the excesses of the Perón years of dictatorial rule. Perón, however, could not last forever. In 1955, after nine years in power, he was driven from office and forced into exile to Spain. (His wife, Evita, had died of uterine cancer at the age of 33 in 1952, a loss from which he never recovered. Following her death, he had become increasingly out of touch and distant from his people. He may actually have bordered on mental collapse.) With Perón's departure, Borges's personal and professional life improved. New opportunities continually presented themselves. He was offered an academic position as professor of English and American Literature at the Faculty of Philosophy and Letters

Unfortunately, Borges never learned how to type, a skill that might have made composing his literary works easier even if he could not actually physically see. When he was able to see, he had always used paper and pen. With the loss of this approach, he was forced to rely on dictating his works. His mother would be among his most important "secretaries." She took notes for him, read to him, and became his eyes and hands. There were others, mostly young women whom he employed at the National Library. The process of Borges composing, then dictating to a second person was a laborious one. It would often take two or three hours to produce a poem or even a half page of prose. Yet his blindness never stopped him from producing, even if the pace of production was dramatically slower than in his younger years.

* Richard Burgin, *Conversations with Jorge Luis Borges* (New York: Holt, Rinehart, and Winston, 1969), 43.

** Ronald Christ, "The Art of Fiction: Jorge Luis Borges," in *Paris Review*, 40, 1967, 120.

at Buenos Aires University. The appointment would be long-term, lasting until 1968.

Along with this plum appointment, Borges, now in his mid-fifties, received another recognition as a literary figure in Argentina. He was appointed director of the National Library, a dramatic step up from the drudgery of his municipal library job. This would be a long-term honor that Borges held for 18 years. The appointment did not require much of Jorge Luis, but he came to work anyway, rarely missing a day. He used his position to reinvent the library as a center for cultural enlightenment through a lecture program and by reviving the library's literary journal. With this appointment, Borges had found a unique place for himself, one that reflected his literary achievements.

All was not well on all fronts, however. His vision was becoming a full-fledged difficulty. Cataracts had continued to plague him through the following decades. He would soon completely lose vision in his left eye, and his right eye presented everything in a hazy blur. By the mid-1950s, he went under the knife for the eighth cataract surgery of his life. His situation was ironic. He was, as he noted in an interview years later, surrounded by "800,000 volumes of the national Library and I have been getting closer to darkness ever since that time."[97]

6

Fame and Marriage

Even as Borges continued to lose his eyesight, he did not stop writing. He did change directions in his subject matter by the mid-1950s, however, returning to poetry. It would be a permanent shift. Poetry had opened his writing career, and it would take him to the end. Over the intervening decades, from the 1950s to 1985, Jorge Luis would write and publish eight books of poetry. It may be that his poor eyesight was directly connected to his return to poetic verse. Since poetry followed established forms and structures dependent on meter, he was able to compose without sight. During his continuing long walks, he would "write" his poems in his head. As he strolled along, Borges claimed he could "carry a sonnet in my head, polishing and altering as I go. You can't do that with a long piece of prose."[98]

His physical impairment would not keep Borges from accomplishing further literary successes. He was still writing, he had his teaching position at the university, and he was lecturing to various audiences on a wide variety of his personal favorite subjects. His mind was still keen, and he was still searching for new avenues of literary growth. To this end, he began studying the ancient languages of Anglo-Saxon and Old Norse. (He believed these languages were a part of his literary and cultural past because his love of the English language and its culture were never dimmed.) He even included a group of interested students in his study.

Yet there was an important change in the way that he "wrote" by the late 1950s. Given his poor eyesight, he was forced to rely increasingly on dictation. His office in the National Library became a center for him to dictate his words through a second party. He was able to produce a book of poetry, *Manual de zoologia fantastica,* by dictating to his friend Margarita Guerrero, with whom he had worked on an earlier work, *Martín Fierro,* in 1953. At home, his mother served as a secretary of sorts, taking down his words and putting them on paper. He soon developed a system for producing his literary pieces. One of those to whom he dictated, a young woman named Maria Esther Vazquez, would later recall Borges's process of writing without the use of pen and paper:

> He dictates five or six words, which initiate a prose piece or the first verse of a poem, and immediately has them read out. As the words come, the index finger of his right hand slides down the back of his left hand, as if it were running over an invisible page. The phrase is repeated once, twice, thrice, four times until he sees how to go on, and he dictates another five or six words. Then he has the whole thing read out. As he dictates with punctuation, that has to be read out too. This fragment is reread, accompanied by hand movements, until he encounters the next phrase.[99]

NEW HONORS

His work continued to bring him respect, recognition, and honors. During the mid-1950s, Cuyo, one of Argentina's most treasured and oldest universities, granted Borges with an honorary doctorate degree. (It would be the first of many he would receive in his lifetime.) Soon after, he received the high honor of the National Prize for literature. Just as he had written about his favorite authors during his younger years, Jorge Luis himself was being written about. He was the study of scholars who wrote books, monographs, and essays that focused on Borges's literary works. For the most part, these works were positive of his literary contributions.

In 1960, he published an eclectic work titled *El hacedor (Dream Tigers).* It was a collection of poetry, literary scenes, short anecdotes, and even parables, or stories that have a moral lesson. The book was an important work for Borges. It was destined to become one of his readers' favorites, as well as one of his own. He later wrote in his "Autobiographical Essay" that it "seems to me my most personal work."[100] In the book's title piece, "Dream Tigers," Borges returns to one of his boyhood fascinations. As a youth, he had seen them in zoos and had drawn countless pictures of these wild Asian beasts. To the adult writer, the tiger had "come to symbolise a lithe, brutal, other reality challenging the temporal everyday."[101] In the piece, Borges claims he has gained the power to "cause a tiger," which he does, even if indistinctly, through the force of his own words.

Perhaps the strangest and most revealing piece in the book was an essay he titled "Borges and I." In this work, he returned to a lifelong fear and psychological hang-up—his dread of being "multiplied," as in reflections in several mirrors. Borges removed himself from himself in the work, writing: "It's to the other man, to Borges, that things happen. . . . I live, I let myself live, so that Borges can weave his tales and poems, and those tales and poems are my justification."[102] Through this essay, Borges appears to have become so self-

(*continues on page 86*)

A CIRCLE OF FRIENDS

FRIENDS, MENTORS, AND COLLABORATORS

Perhaps one of the most important aspects of Jorge Borges's literary career is that he created many of his works of poetry and fiction with the help of a long list of friends and comrades. It makes sense, of course, that he was reliant on others to produce his literature, if for no reason other than his poor eyesight. For decades he depended on those whom he called friends to read to him, to collaborate with in writing, to dictate his works to (once he had fallen into near blindness), and otherwise share life with.

It was not something he was good at as a youth. He often had trouble making friends as a schoolboy because he was so different, someone to be mocked and bullied as a dandy and a reader. Yet by the time he was in his late teens and early twenties, Borges was almost constantly surrounded by a group of those like him or at least those who appreciated him. He always recalled how he had received support from his male schoolmates in Geneva while he struggled to take tests in French.

Some of these emotional associates would have profound impacts on Borges and his career as a writer. Early on, there were the mentors, such as his father's friend and old school chum, Evaristo Carriego. Other mentor-friends include Rafael Cansinos-Assens and Macedonio Ferdandez, another older friend of his father, who would guide Borges into the school of ultraism.

By the early 1920s, he was surrounded by many literary friends, including the poets Ricardo Guiraldes and Alfredo Brandan Caraffa and the novelist Palo Rojas Paz. Guiraldes would become a special friend and guide concerning Borges's writings. By the late 1920s, he had found literary camaraderie in Alejandro Schulz Soleri and Carlos Mastronardi, with whom he shared his long walks through the back streets of Buenos Aires and its suburbs. Not all his writing friends were male. Victoria Ocampo, whom Borges met in 1925, would have great artistic impact on the Argentine writer.

Others would come along in later decades, such as his good friend Nestor Ibarra, who first translated Borges's works into French, opening up his literary career to a non-Spanish-speaking audience. Ibarra also shared those long walks with Borges. Then, Borges met one of his most important lifelong friends and literary collaborators, Adolfo Bioy Casares. They would share conversations over the decades and even collaborated on works, such as the detective parodies.

As Borges drifted into middle age and then his elderly years, he relied on the friendships of women, several of whom were much younger but who served as emotional supports even as they aided his writing. Yet even as Borges found friendship with such women, providing him with stimulus of an intellectual and literary nature, they also stimulated his physical side. These women typically functioned first as friends with whom Borges held something in common, especially his art. Yet remaining with them on a level that went no further than mutual appreciation for the literary was sometimes, even for the sexually quirky Jorge Luis, impossible.

Such women might become the true objects of his immature affections. On such occasions, Borges was typically at his most awkward, struggling to find a way to kiss one here or embrace one there, revealing his split personality when it came to sexual matters. He would sometimes rush into a relationship, head over heels in love with the thought of a given woman, only to find himself repulsed by the intricacies of lovemaking.

Of those women who drifted in and out of his life, some remaining within his sphere for several years, one of the most significant was Estela Canto, to whom he would propose marriage, only to be turned down. They, too, walked throughout the neighborhoods of Buenos Aires. Margarita Guerrero, Maria Esther Vazquez, Elsa Astete Millan, and Maria Kodama would become not only good companions, but they worked as his secretary—collaborating, taking dictation, and even marrying (as with Elsa and Maria) the elderly Argentine writer.

These friendships were crucial to the founding, development, advancement, and establishment of the literary career that would become Jorge Luis Borges's legacy.

(*continued from page 83*)

conscious of his literary success and fame that he was forced to view himself abstractly, taking on a separate identity. He began to frequently refer to himself in the third person would become a common way for him to refer to himself. Some of this was simply a joke he chose to play on himself, but, during many of his later interviews, he often spoke as if "Borges, the literary figure" was an entirely different person.

NEW FAME ABROAD

By the 1960s, Jorge Luis Borges was on the verge of becoming an international literary star. He had been translated into French as early as the 1940s, but it would not be until 1961 that true worldwide fame was his. That year, he won the Formentor Prize, an international honor given by a group of six prestigious publishers with a cash prize of $10,000. (That year, the group split the prize between Borges and French author Samuel Beckett.) While honor and money had their own value, they would only manage to prime the pump for Borges. Suddenly, almost immediately, he was known around the world. He was soon translated into English. His earlier work *Ficciónes* was translated into several languages.

The University of Texas invited Borges to take a position at the university as a lecturer. He agreed, accompanied by his mother. Borges was soon the darling of American academics. (The bachelor Borges and his mother, Leonor, were often mistaken for either brother and sister or husband and wife.) His writings were admired for their unique qualities, especially his experimental fiction, which set him apart from a host of other South American writers of the first half of the twentieth century. He was also admired by a new generation of American writers of the 1960s, including Thomas Pynchon, Donald Barthelme, and John Barth. Inspired by his style, these writers produced their own brands of experimental works, including short stories and novels. As he toured the United States, visiting New York, Massachusetts, and

Despite his failing eyesight, Borges continued to produce an enormous body of work. In the mid-1950s, he returned to writing poetry, and in the following three decades, he published eight books of poetry. His keen mind and boundless energy saw him continue to lecture and tour throughout the world.

New Mexico, Borges made a positive impression. His "combination of conservative dress, courteous manners, and sharp wit intrigued his audiences. He was perceived as an exotic figure."[103] Jorge Luis praised Americans for their "generosity and friendliness."[104]

Everything Borges touched was turning to gold. Honors and recognition poured in from around the world, especially from his homeland. The government elected him to the Argentine Academy of Letters. (The French government soon presented him with their equivalent of that national honor.) Requests for visits and lectures came to him regularly, leading to a European visit in 1963 (again with Leonor) that included London, Paris, Geneva, and Madrid. Nearly 50 years had passed since his first visit to Europe, and this trip gave him opportunity to reconnect with some old friends, including Cansinos-Assens, Borges's old mentor, then 81 years old.

During this tour, his mother received nearly as much attention as he did. She was, despite her age, still an active, stylish woman with modern tastes who projected herself well with the media. She became the darling to the journalists who reported on the mother and son duo. With constant press and academic recognition, Jorge Luis was now utterly famous, with no opportunity to turn away from almost constant recognition. He was making more money than ever before. Yet both fame and fortune were to have an immediate, negative effect on the middle-aged writer. Between the tours, the lectures, the attention, and the press, he was also writing less and less.

A CHANGE OF PARTNERS

Borges followed up his 1963 European tour with a second tour to the continent the following year and a tour to several South American countries in 1965. By this time, however, he was no longer traveling with his mother, who was approaching 90 years of age. Instead, he made these tours with Maria Esther Vazquez, then only 23 years old. She had previously done dictation for Jorge Luis for a few years at the National Library. Maria Esther was an intelligent woman and a great admirer of the Argentine icon. The difference in age allowed her to look at Borges for what he was to the rest of the world—an elderly writer of great talent and creativity. Years later, she admitted to thinking of Borges as being "as old as the Pyramids."[105] It probably never occurred to her, until it was too late, that her mentor might fall in love with her.

The second European tour included a visit to Berlin, Copenhagen, and Stockholm (with honors received in the latter two cities). Borges also visited Paris, where he lectured on Shakespeare in a celebration of the 400th anniversary of the great writer's birth. (Borges delivered the lecture, titled "Shakespeare and Us," in French, which had been translated for him from Spanish. He had memorized the entire speech by listening over and over to a tape recording of it, leaving his audience with the impression he was speaking extemporaneously.) Borges also returned to England at the invitation of the British Council. After he and Maria Esther returned to Argentina, they worked together on a pair of literary projects, including a work on German literature and a Spanish-language text on English literature. By this time, the elderly author was intent in his feelings for his younger associate. Despite his age, he still longed to marry, to have a woman other than his mother to look after him. Yet before he asked her to marry him, he found out she was already engaged. This news drove Borges to despair. He was so upset and distraught, he "went to the dentist, and had his teeth pulled out. It seemed the only solution to his distress."[106]

Borges managed to bounce back from his emotional loss. In 1964, he published a collection of poems, *Obra poetica*, some of which were drawn from *Dream Tigers*. He also engaged in additional writing projects, usually with young women who likely helped him recover from his loneliness and despair at having "lost" Maria Esther. He collaborated with his old companion Bioy on another clever detective story. That fall, he took his tour to Chile and Columbia with Esther Zemborain de Torres Duggan, whom Borges had known for 20 years. She was "a frail, Anglophile woman, married to a boozy, somewhat abusive Basque [from the northern region of Spain]."[107] She was just the type of woman to which Borges was always attracted. Yet she was a dedicated Catholic, married, and not the answer to Jorge Luis's continuing loneliness. That personal problem was to be answered by yet another woman.

As the 1960s progressed, Jorge Luis's career continued on its stellar course. In 1966, he published a new poetry collection. Borges also published a story in 1967, "his first substantial tale since 1953, but very different in style and preoccupation from those of the *Ficciónes* and *Aleph* years."[108] He first dictated the work to Leonor in 1966. The story was titled *La intrusa (The Intruder),* a dark story of a pair of brothers who sexually shared the same lover, then sold her to a brothel, only to then murder her. Despite the stark subject matter, Borges came to think of the work as one of his best.

MARRIAGE AT LAST

Despite the heights of his literary successes and recognitions, the pang of loneliness never fully left the elderly Borges. Even in his late sixties, he still considered the possibilities of marrying for the first time. He would do so with a woman he had first met more than 40 years earlier, when she was 17 years old. Her name was Elsa Astete Millán. Borges had even considered marrying her then, but she had married another, Ricardo Albarracin, a friend of Jorge Luis's. Albarracin was now dead, the victim of lung cancer, and Elsa was alone, perhaps as alone as Borges. He had sent her a pair of letters more than 20 years earlier, telling her how he still loved her, but the communication had gone nowhere. It was now 1967, and he paid a visit to her. Within a few months, they married. At first, mother Leonor was not excited about the match, feeling Elsa was not educated enough for her son, but she soon softened and accepted her, telling her son, "I think it'll suit you better to marry Elsa, because she's a widow, and already knows about life."[109]

What exactly did Jorge Luis Borges expect his marriage to be like? After all, he was almost 68 years old, and she was 20 years younger. Borges had spoken confidently to friends, saying, "I need a home."[110] There would be a routine about

In his late sixties, Borges married for the first time. He is shown here with his wife, Elsa Astete Millán, in January 1968, months after their marriage. The marriage did not last, however, and in 1970, the couple divorced.

the relationship. She woke him every morning, drew his bath, made his breakfast, and packed him off to work at the National Library. They ate every evening meal with the Bioys. If, indeed, Borges had finally found a woman to rely on instead of his mother, the marriage was little more than that. Borges would always remain a man who needed someone to take care of him. There was little else he expected of Elsa, and the marriage would not work. From the beginning, they slept in separate bedrooms. As a friend of Borges's would note, "The problem was Borges and Elsa had nothing in common."[111]

Fortunately, Borges had other outlets. Within a month of the marriage, he was off to America with Elsa, where he accepted the post of Charles Eliot Norton Poetry Chair at Harvard University. There, he delivered a series of lectures titled "The Craft of Verse." (Borges did write a poem to his new bride while at Harvard, titled "Elsa.") He remained in the United States for seven months, during which time he traveled extensively. He took in the literary sights in and around Boston, paying visits to Nathaniel Hawthorne's Salem, Ralph Waldo Emerson's Concord, Herman Melville's New Bedford, Emily Dickinson's Amherst, and "to Longfellow's around the corner from where I lived."[112] He also traveled as far away as Missouri, Illinois, and Iowa. He did so much traveling and speaking at other academic institutions that Harvard officials became angry with him, thinking he was missing too many lectures in Cambridge.

It was at Harvard that Borges met a young man half his age who would have a profound impact on his life and ultimate legacy as a writer. Norman Thomas di Giovanni was an Italian-American who worked as a translator near Boston. At the time of Borges's visit to Harvard, di Giovanni was working on a bilingual anthology of Latin-American poetry. He had only recently discovered Borges when he came across one of the Argentine writer's poems. When he realized Borges was visiting Harvard, he wrote to him asking to translate a book of Jorge Luis's poems. Borges had already heard of di Giovanni and his work from mutual associates at Harvard and agreed to meet him. They hit it off immediately, as di Giovanni would later write, "That visit . . . has never ended. Borges and I liked each other, we enjoyed the work, and it was the right hour to have come knocking . . . I had become the last American to discover Borges and the first to work with him."[113] Almost immediately, the two men became friends, and di Giovanni was destined to become Borges's primary translator for years. Together they would work through Borges's "last great and productive period of work."[114]

7

The Last Years

Di Giovanni convinced Borges to write about a dozen poems so he could add them to existing poetry for a new book. The work, published on Borges's seventieth birthday, was titled *In Praise of Darkness.* In it, Borges confronts his blindness, old age, and issues of ethics. Borges was so thrilled with the work they had accomplished that he and di Giovanni agreed, under contract, to collaborate as poet and translator on eight more poetry collections. This surge of literary output came at a crucial time for Borges. Depressed by his marriage and distracted by his lecture tours, his writing had fallen off dramatically. He was suddenly back on track. He recovered from his emotional struggles, found new confidence, and put pen to paper. As biographer James Woodall wrote, "Borges the married man had become a writer again."[115]

A FAILING MARRIAGE

In addition to 1969's poetry, Borges published a collection of 11 new short stories, *Doctor Brodie's Report.* These new fictions were, perhaps, less experimental than earlier story collections, such as *Ficciónes* and *El Aleph*, but they represented good work by Borges, coming late in his life. Such new literary output brought an invitation to lecture at the University of Oklahoma. This time, however, basically at the suggestion of di Giovanni, Borges did not lecture on his writing or on literature otherwise. Instead, he talked about his personal life. This was an important redirection for Borges, and he returned home to Buenos Aires to retool his lectures in a publication titled "Autobiographical Essay." It became an important work for Borges and Borges biographers. *New Yorker* magazine paid $9,000 to print the lengthy biography.

Three years had passed, and his marriage to Elsa had fallen into complete disarray. Borges came to understand that his marriage was "an unaccountable mistake, a huge mistake. . . . A quite unexplainable and mysterious mistake."[116] Yet even in his early seventies, Borges was still, in many ways, an immature man who struggled with his emotions. He could not bring himself to speak directly to Elsa about their relationship (or lack of one), which finally led to a strange solution:

> Borges never mustered the courage, or found the courtesy, to talk to Elsa. Instead, he planned a day of escape. One morning after breakfast, on his way out of the house, Elsa asked him what he would like for lunch, and he told her, *puchero* [a type of stew], one of his favorite meals. However, that afternoon Borges did not come home for lunch. Instead, five men showed up, two lawyers with legal orders for separation (under Argentine law, divorce was not possible under these circumstances) and three movers to take away Borges's belongings.[117]

Elsa was stunned at the dismissive way she was finally treated by Borges, an insult for which she never forgave him. Borges moved back into the home of his aged mother, Leonor.

A TRAVELING MAN

While his personal life had been dismal for years, Borges continued to experience triumph in his professional career. He was a sightless man who was constantly in motion, taking trips everywhere to lecture and receive various honors. He was given the Inter-American prize for Literature in Brazil, with a cash award of $25,000. Only when his mother became ill did he cut the trip short. Leonor was now in her nineties and had struggled with poor health for several years. Some biographers of Borges suggest that she may have experienced a rapid decline in her quality of life following his marriage to Elsa. It was during those three years that Leonor watched as her son's needs were being met by another woman, resulting in her belief that she no longer had a purpose in life. Nevertheless, Borges did not remain tied to his mother but continued to travel, returning to the United States and making a trip to the Middle East. On such trips, di Giovanni and his wife always accompanied Borges. The aging Argentine returned to Britain (where he received an honorary degree from Oxford) and Scotland, and di Giovanni even surprised him with a trip to Iceland. There, Borges could take up his studies of Anglo-Saxon again, as well as Old Norse, which he did by reading Icelandic sagas.

Through his travels, Borges was almost constantly praised for his literary achievements. On one occasion, however, he met criticism that led to a direct confrontation. While speaking at Columbia University in New York City, a lecture that featured several Latin-American writers and intellectuals, Borges was criticized for not being overtly political in his writings. He was accused of avoiding the important political issues of the times. Jorge Luis defended himself by implying that another man's "revolution" did not have to be his own. Puerto Rican students standing at the back of the lecture hall began protesting against the university's alleged racist

On one of Borges's many overseas trips, he was awarded an honorary doctorate of letters from Oxford University, England, in 1970. By that time, Borges had become an international celebrity, whose fame and influence in the world of literature was most likely greater than any other twentieth-century writer.

policies. In the excitement, one screamed a curse at Borges, which in Spanish is a direct insult at one's mother, specifically referring to her as a prostitute. Blind and about 70 years old, Borges became enraged. He rapped his cane hard on a desk and challenged the young student to a duel. The scene was eventually calmed, but Borges was emotionally outraged by the incident.

It was not that Borges did not hold political views. It was that his politics often remained understated and were rarely an overt agenda of his writing. Additionally, his political opinions tended to be conservative, which did not sit well with the many Latin-American writers whose politics leaned to the liberal left. (Borges was so politically conservative and such an admirer of President Richard Nixon that he dedicated his Spanish translation of Whitman's *Leaves of Grass* to the American leader.) Basically, however, politics was not where Borges tended to live. He was a writer, one who was able to remain above much of the world "in an ivory tower of literature and language."[118]

One political event that Borges was not able to make himself remain above occurred in 1973 when Perón was reelected to the presidency of Argentina. During the 18 years since his exile to Spain in 1955, Argentina had struggled under poor leaders, violence, and political struggle as governments toppled like card houses. For some, Perón's return to power was an opportunity to breath. Borges, however, could not accept the return of the old president he had despised for decades. In protest, he quit his position at the National Library and began speaking out against Perón. He became so obsessed with Perón that he was probably unable or unwilling to realize even the positive programs that the Argentine leader instituted, including social welfare and labor reforms.

Borges would not be alone in his opposition to Perón, but even his old comrades in SADE accepted the return of the earlier leader to power. While Borges did not believe he was putting himself in jeopardy by speaking out overtly and vehemently against Perón, in fact, he began receiving menacing calls at home. When Leonor received one such call, and the caller threatened to kill her, she coolly gave him her address and told the faceless threat that he had better hurry over "as she was ninety-eight years old and would not last long."[119] On another occasion, someone actually did place a bomb outside Borges's apartment building. Although it failed to go off, Borges did respond to the threat, chastising the perpetrators as cowards. Perón himself did not last long, however, dying on July 1, 1974. Borges did not mourn his death, even though the decade that followed Perón would be politically miserable for Argentina.

BORGES REMAINS IN MOTION

The verbal attack at Columbia did not sway Borges from making additional trips to the United States throughout the 1970s and into the 1980s. From 1972 to 1976, he visited and lectured at the University of New Hampshire, in Houston, at the University of Michigan, and at the University of Maine. (Di Giovanni spent four years working with Borges and finally left his mentor in 1972. Seven years would pass before the two men saw one another again.) Borges traveled abroad to other countries, including a visit to Israel in 1971. Borges was always a strong advocate and admirer of Israel, even though it placed him, again, on the wrong side of many leftist Latin-American writers. During the late 1970s to mid-1980s, the Argentine writer visited Egypt, Japan, Moroco, Germany, Great Britain, Ecuador, and Puerto Rico. In addition, he visited the United States and Spain 11 times each. During the late 1960s and throughout the 1970s, Borges was also giving many interviews. He enjoyed such dialogues, yet he often tried to turn an interviewer's questions about him and his work into a discussion of the works of his favorite writers.

All would not remain a matter of touring, lecturing, and finding the time to write. Great changes were still to come to Jorge Luis Borges in his later years. It was difficult for him when di Giovanni left in 1972. His mother's health continued to decline, and she finally died in 1975 at the age of 99. Her death would rank among the most significant losses of his life. He had, after all, lived with his mother for nearly all of his 76 years. She had been his primary caregiver from his youth to his old age.

Yet even before Leonor's death, another woman had entered his life. When di Giovanni left Borges in 1972, the Argentine writer began working closely with another collaborator, a younger woman of Argentine and Japanese descent. She was Maria Kodama, whom Borges had met when she was only 12 years old, when her father had brought her to one of the writer's lectures in 1958. In the years since, she had gone on to earn a doctorate in English at the University of Buenos Aires. It was there that she met Borges a second time on terms closer to being equal. (She had been one of the students with whom he had studied Anglo-Saxon and Old Norse.) She and Borges had become close friends, and she had even tagged along with him and di Giovanni on the Iceland trip.

Kodama would become his constant companion. From 1972 to 1985, Borges and Maria traveled frequently together. She helped him put together, in 1974, the book *Obras completas*, a compilation of most of his poetry and all of his prose to date. It was a massive work, adding up to 1,200 pages, and it was a popular and successful publication. There were other works, including a book of poetry, *El libro de arena (The Book of Sand)*, that he published following Leonor's death.

Biographers have speculated about the exact nature of the relationship between Maria Kodama and Borges. She was decades younger, but great distances in age had never kept Borges from considering an emotional relationship or even marriage as out of the question. It is doubtful that Maria and Jorge Luis ever had a sexual relationship. Maria was an important friend to Borges, and the timing of that relationship was likely quite crucial to the aging writer. It came just as he was losing di Giovanni and his mother and Perón was coming

Maria Kodama was Borges's secretary, traveling companion, and in later years, his wife. Kodama is shown here at an exhibition in Rome, Italy, in 2000, honoring the one-hundredth anniversary of her husband's birth. Kodama is a writer, translator, and professor of literature.

back to power. Borges came to rely on Kodama for friendship, companionship, conversation, collaboration, and emotional support.

POLITICAL TRAPS

During Borges's final decade, he continued to write and even found himself at the center of new controversies, including political ones. Following Perón's death in 1974, his wife,

Isabel, took the reins of power, only to be toppled by the military two years later. Borges was so anti-Perónist that he gladly accepted the new leader, General Jorge Videla, who, as things turned out, would rule Argentina with a bloody hand. During his days in power, the government engaged in the kidnappings (called the *desaparecidos*, or "the disappeared") of dozens of left-wing opponents every week. In the early days of the general's regime, Borges even shared lunch with him, "declaring afterwards his junta to be gentlemen."[120] In part, Borges support of Videla was driven by his rejection of socialism and his fear of communism. In his heart, he was really a supporter of no government at all, an anarchist, who dreamed "of having no government, having no police force, of being a kind people different from what we are now." Yet the time was never right for actual anarchy, and a strong military hand like Videla's would be, to Borges, "a necessary evil."[121] Nevertheless, his support of Videla drew the angry condemnation of the left, both in Argentina and abroad.

There were other serious political missteps made by the elderly Borges. He paid a call on another South American military dictator, General Augusto Pinochet of Chile. He also made an unfortunate statement about Argentina's history in which he declared that his country's founders had been "wise to use the remnants of black slaves as cannon-fodder, that it was a historical achievement to have rid the country of its native Indians, and it was only to be regretted that the seeds of ignorance had survived to allow for the growth of Perónism."[122] Such errors in judgment cost Borges dearly. There were cancellations of scheduled appearances, including a planned honor of his life's achievements by a Spanish magazine. Perhaps, most importantly, officials in Stockholm who had been considering him for a Nobel Prize in literature dropped their plans. It was an honor he never received.

In time, Borges understood the Videla regime for what it was, and he turned against the government, even signing an

(*continues on page 104*)

JORGE LUIS BORGES'S LEGACY

CREATING AN UMBRELLA OF GREAT LITERATURE

Jorge Luis Borges read and wrote with the greatest of passions. Reading and writing was the centerpiece of his life. They were his reason for living. While others might find meaning in painting, sculpting, and the performance or decorative arts, Borges managed to find meaning in his literary endeavors. He created for himself a unique domestic world, dominated by his overbearing mother, whom he nevertheless loved dearly, and then by unconventional marriages. Borges remained childless, never producing a new generation of his family line. Yet he parented through his literary efforts by producing heirs to his fertile mind and his creative juices. Jorge Luis Borges created, through a 60-year-long career, one of the most significant and enduring literary legacies of any writer of the twentieth century.

The scope of his legacy was planetary. His works came to be read, even before he had become an elderly, statesman-like writer, around the world, and the reach of that spread of his poetry, his stories, and his essays was enormous. His writings had intercontinental impact with readers from America to Asia—the New World to the Old—and it is no wonder. This was due, in part, to the fact that even before he created works for an international audience, he first absorbed the literature of those countries that would adopt his writings.

During his lifetime, he was much more than a passing fan of English, French, German, Italian, Scandinavian, and American literature. He was a student and a scholar, reading the works of other continents with a great passion. He was able to take what he had learned from others and spin it into tales that were so new that they appeared to his international audiences as if they were created from something quite mysterious. Even though Borges is viewed as a writer by his nationality—he is counted among the most important Argentine writers—he did not write in a way that was bound by borders. His themes were about the intricacies of human existence, which defy limitation and being pigeonholed by the most widely read of his critics.

The result was a legacy of written art that would often defy categorization, or even accurate description. Yet through his works, he managed to bring the literatures of other places and other centuries under one canopy. He created an umbrella of modern writing that drew readers like moths during his lifetime and that will, one suspects, withstand the scrutiny of centuries to follow.

This legacy of Borges—that he was able to extend his literary efforts beyond those of a mere "regional" or "national" writer—lifts him up above so many other writers who make up the group of great literary geniuses. He moved beyond the confines of being just an Argentine author by literally moving beyond Argentina's borders. If Borges was a great writer, he was first a great traveler. Throughout his life, even beginning in his youth, he moved from continent to continent, learning the ways of each nationality and ethnic group he encountered. The result was that he not only wrote about others and their unique worlds, but he understood those worlds because he had lived within each one.

He managed to accomplish all this without the usual bravado and cause campaigning that often accompanies other writers who become famous. Through it all, the books, the lectures, and the honors, Borges remained grounded and conventional, even timid. In fact, he often referred to himself in the third person as if "being Borges" was more than he was capable of understanding. That Borges had strong beliefs, that he held some causes dear to himself, and that he wanted to accomplish great ends through his literary output is certain.

Today, a generation removed from the life of Jorge Luis Borges, the works of Argentina's greatest writer continue to teach. His voice continues to speak through his millions of words and the message is clear: "It is that the human imagination, that making capacity of the inner world, is still worth a lifetime's dedication."*

* James Woodall, *Borges, A Life* (New York: BasicBooks, 1996), 260.

(*continued from page 101*)

open letter opposed to the thousands of desaparecidos. While the politics of his homeland proved complicated for Borges, he did not generally go out of his way to become embroiled in such contemporary events. He was approaching 80 years of age, had lived a full life, and had written on nearly every subject of his interest and passion. For that, he wrote little during the 1980s, even as the honors and awards continued for his life's accumulated works. (He penned his last story in 1982, *La memoria de Shakespeare [Shakespeare's Memory].)* He and Maria continued to travel, and they collaborated on a book of their wanderings, with Borges providing the travelogue and Maria snapping the photographs that illustrated the work. In one of her photos, the blind octogenarian is seen touching a tiger.

Illness dogged his later years. Although he was healthy throughout most of his life, he had prostate surgery at age 79. By then, he was also diabetic. By the mid-1980s, he was diagnosed with liver cancer and chose to leave his homeland. Due to the politics, he refused to die on Argentine soil. He returned to Geneva, the city in which he had grown into adulthood for it "was as much home to him as Buenos Aires."[123] It was there that Borges and Maria married on April 24, 1986. He was 87, and she was 40. The marriage was technically awkward because he had never divorced his first wife, Elsa. Divorce was not then lawful in Argentina. To fix the problem, the marriage license was applied for in Paraguay, where a divorce could be obtained. Many in the Borges family, including his sister and her children, opposed the union. There was a fear that this younger woman might manage to inherit the rights to all of Borges's writings. (Indeed, at Jorge Luis's death, Maria did become the sole heir.)

The matter of an old marriage and a new divorce would soon matter little for Jorge Luis Borges. Just eight weeks following his marriage to Maria, Borges died on a Saturday morning, June 14, 1986. Although Jorge Luis was not a religious man, he received blessings from a Catholic priest the previous evening. The funeral was held in the cathedral of Saint-Pierre, located in the older part of Geneva where Borges had lived as a youth. He was buried in the cemetery of Plainpalais in Geneva. To local residents, the burial site was known as the cemetery des Rois, or "of the Kings." It was a fitting resting place for the author who had reigned as a lion of twentieth-century literature.

Chronology

1899 Jorge Luis Borges born August 24, Buenos Aires, Argentina.

1914 Goes to Geneva, Switzerland. Remains four years, attending private schools.

1919 Leaves Geneva for Spain, where earliest poems are published.

1921 Returns with family to Buenos Aires; begins to develop literary career, working with several magazines.

1923 Publishes first book of poetry, *Fervor de Buenos Aires.*

1923–1924 Travels to Europe.

1925 Publishes second book of poetry, *Luna de Enfrente,* and first collection of essays, *Inquisiciónes.*

1926–1928 Publishes books of essays, *El Tamaño de mi esperanza* and *El idioma de los argentinos.*

1899 – **1956**

- **1899** Jorge Luis Borges born August 24 in Buenos Aires, Argentina
- **1923** Publishes first book of poetry, *Fervor de Buenos Aires*
- **1930** Publishes *Evaristo Carriego*
- **1937** Begins job in a branch of the Municipal Library
- **1939** Publishes "Pierre Menard," his first "Borgesian" tale
- **1949** Publishes important work *The Aleph*
- **1955** Appointed Director of the National Library
- **1956** Receives the National Prize for Literature

1929 Takes second place in the Buenos Aires municipal literary contest; publishes book of poetry, *Cauderno San Martín.*

1930 Publishes *Evaristo Carriego.*

1932 Publishes *Discusión.*

1933 Becomes editor of *Critica.*

1935 English grandmother, Frances Haslam de Borges, dies; publishes *Historia universal de la infamia.*

1936 Publishes essay collection, *Historia de la eternidad.*

1937–1946 Serves as First Assistant in a branch of the Municipal Library.

1938 Falls in an accident, becomes ill, and nearly dies; father dies.

1961 **1986**

1961 Receives Formentor Prize

1967 Marries his first wife, Elsa Astete Millán. Teaches at Harvard University

1971 Receives honorary degrees from Columbia and Oxford Universities

1975 Mother, Leonor, dies

1981 Receives honorary doctorate from Harvard University

1985 Moves to Geneva, Switzerland

1986 Marries Maria Kodama. Dies June 14

1939 Publishes "Pierre Menard," a story critics would consider the first truly "Borgesian" tale.

1942 Collaborates with Adolfo Bioy-Casares on a story titled "Six Problems for Don Isidro Parodi."

1946 With rise of Perón to power, quits his library job.

1949 Publishes the seminal work, *The Aleph.*

1950 Elected president of SADE.

1951 *Ficciónes* is published in Paris in French.

1952 Publishes *Otras inquisiciónes.*

1955 With fall of Perón from power, appointed Director of the National Library; by this time, he is nearly blind.

1956–1968 Serves as professor of English and American literature at the University of Buenos Aires; in 1956, receives the National Prize for Literature.

1957 Collaborates with Margarita Guerrero on *Manual de zoologia fantastica.*

1960 Publishes *El hacedor.*

1961 Receives Formentor Prize.

1962 English versions of *Labyrinths* and *Ficciónes* are published.

1963 Travels extensively throughout Europe.

1964 Publishes collection of poems, *El Otro, el mismo.*

1967 Marries first wife, Elsa Astete Millán; teaches at Harvard University.

1968 Publishes *El libro de los seres imaginarios.* Meets di Giovanni.

1969 Publishes *Elogio de la sombra.*

1970 Publishes *El informe de Brodie.*

1971 Receives honorary degrees from Columbia University and Oxford University.

1972 Publishes *El oro de los tigres.*

1973 Following return of Perón presidency, resigns directorship of National Library.

1974 Finishes *Obras completas.*

1975 Mother, Leonor, dies.

1976 Co-authors another detective novel parody with Bioy.

1977 Publishes *Historia de la noche*, a collection of poems.

1979 Travels to Japan, Germany, and Iceland, receiving honors and awards from their governments.

1980 Travels to Spain.

1981 Receives honorary doctorate from Harvard University.

1984 Publishes *Atlas.*

1985 Moves to Geneva, Switzerland.

1986 Marries Maria Kodama; dies June 14.

Notes

Introduction

1 Emir Rodriguez Monegal, *Jorge Luis Borges: A Literary Biography* (New York: E.P. Dutton, 1978), 4.
2 Amy Sickels, "Biography of Jorge Luis Borges" in *Jorge Luis Borges*. Edited by Harold Bloom (Philadelphia: Chelsea House Publishers, 2004), 8.
3 Edwin Williamson, *Borges, A Life* (New York: Viking Penguin, 2004) p. 4.
4 Ibid.
5 Jorge Luis Borges, "An Autobiographical Essay," in the *Aleph and Other Stories, 1933–1969* (New York: Dutton, 1970), 208.
6 James Woodall, *Borges, A Life* (New York: BasicBooks, 1996), 177.

Chapter 1

7 Jason Wilson, *Jorge Luis Borges* (London: Reaktion Books, 2006), 20.
8 Monegal, 3.
9 Borges, *Essay*, 204–205.
10 Sickels, 8.
11 Borges, *Essay*, 209.
12 Wilson, 27.
13 Sickels, 8.
14 Ibid., 9.
15 Jorge Luis Borges, *Evaristo Carriego* (Buenos Aires: Emece Editores, 1955), 9.
16 Wilson, 22.
17 Sickels, 9.
18 Monegal, 37.
19 Sickels, 9.
20 Woodall, 15.
21 Ibid., 14.
22 Sickels, 10.
23 Woodall, 19.
24 Ibid.
25 Monegal, 92.

Chapter 2

26 Sickels, 11.
27 Borges, *Essay*, p. 214.
28 Ibid., 215.
29 Monegal, p. 117.
30 Ibid.
31 Woodall, 27.
32 Wilson, 36.
33 Sickels, 13.
34 Gloria Alcorta, "Entretiens avec Gloria Alcorta," in *L'Herne* (Paris, 1964), 412.
35 Woodall, 34.
36 Ibid., 35.
37 Borges, *Essay*, 218–219.
38 Sickels, 13.
39 Woodall, 38.
40 Borges, *Essay*, 222.
41 Wilson, 47.
42 Sickels, 14.
43 Monegal, 165.

Chapter 3

44 Ibid., 48.
45 Ibid., 49.
46 Borges, *Essay*, 223.
47 Monegal, 168.
48 Borges, *Essay*, 223–224.
49 Ibid., 234.
50 Ibid.
51 Monegal, 169.
52 Borges, *Essay*, 234.
53 Ibid., 227.
54 Woodall, 52.
55 Monegal, 171.
56 Borges, *Essay*, 224.
57 Woodall, 58.
58 Wilson, 60.
59 Jorge Luis Borges, *The Spanish Language in South America—A Literary Problem/ El Gaucho Martín Fierro* (London: Canning House, 1964), 10.
60 Woodall, 70.
61 Ibid., 71.

Chapter 4

62 Sickels, 18.
63 Woodall, 76.
64 Ibid.
65 Ibid., 77.
66 Sickels, 19.
67 Ibid.

68 Woodall, 83.
69 Sickels, 20.
70 Woodall, 88.
71 Ibid., 89.
72 Ibid.
73 Ibid., 103.
74 Monegal, 255.
75 Woodall, 96.
76 Monegal, 101.
77 Sickels, 22.
78 Wilson, 101.
79 Woodall, 104.
80 Borges, *Essay*, 240.
81 Woodall, 105.
82 Ibid.
83 Borges, *Essay*, 242.
84 Woodall, 109–110.

Chapter 5

85 Woodall, 111.
86 Sickels, 25.
87 Ibid., 25–26.
88 Ronald Christ, "The Art of Fiction: Jorge Luis Borges," in *Paris Review*, 40, 1967), 133.
89 Woodall, 133.
90 Ibid., 136.
91 Ibid., 139.
92 Ibid., 145.
93 Williamson, 287.
94 Sickels, 30.
95 Woodall, 402.
96 Ibid., 165.
97 Richard Burgin, *Conversations with Jorge Luis Borges* (New York: Holt, Rinehart, and Winston, 1969), 43.

Chapter 6

98 Ibid., 44.
99 Woodall, 183.
100 Ibid., 188.
101 Ibid.
102 Sickels, 34.
103 Ibid., 35.
104 Ibid., 36.
105 Woodall, 204.
106 Ibid., 208.
107 Ibid.
108 Ibid., 209.
109 Ibid., 214.
110 Ibid., 213.
111 Ibid., 219.
112 Monegal, 450.
113 Woodall, 218.
114 Sickels, 40.

Chapter 7

115 Woodall, 223.
116 Ibid., 230.
117 Sickels, 41.
118 Ibid., 44.
119 Woodall, 246.
120 Ibid., 251.
121 Burgin, 224.
122 Woodall, 251.
123 Ibid., 257.

Bibliography

BOOKS AND MAGAZINES

Alazraki, Jaime. *Jorge Luis Borges.* New York: Columbia University Press, 1971.

Alcorta, Gloria. "Entretiens avec Gloria Alcorta," in *L'Herne,* Paris, 1964.

Bloom, Harold, ed. *Jorge Luis Borges.* New York: Chelsea House Publishers, 1986.

Borges, Jorge Luis. "An Autobiographical Essay," in the *Aleph and Other Stories, 1933–1969.* New York: Dutton, 1970.

———. *Evaristo Carriego.* Buenos Aires: Emece Editores, 1955.

———. *The Spanish Language in South America—A Literary Problem/ El Gaucho Martín Fierro.* London: Canning House, 1964

———. *This Craft of Verse.* Cambridge: Harvard University Press, 2000.

Burgin, Richard. *Conversations with Jorge Luis Borges.* New York: Holt, Rinehart, and Winston, 1969.

Christ, Ronald. "The Art of Fiction: Jorge Luis Borges," in *Paris Review,* 40, 1967.

Di Giovanni, Norman Thomas; Daniel Halpern; and Frank MacShane. *Borges on Writing.* New York: E.P. Dutton & Co., Inc., 1973.

Monegal, Emir Rodriguez. *Jorge Luis Borges: A Literary Biography.* New York: E.P. Dutton, 1978.

Racz, Gregary J., ed. *Jorge Luis Borges (1899–1986) as Writer and Social Critic.* Lewiston, NY: The Edwin Mellen Press, 2003.

Sickels, Amy. "Biography of Jorge Luis Borges," in *Jorge Luis Borges.* Edited by Harold Bloom. Philadelphia: Chelsea House Publishers, 2004.

Williamson, Edwin. *Borges, A Life.* New York: Viking Penguin, 2004.

Wilson, Jason. *Jorge Luis Borges.* London: Reaktion Books, 2006.

Woodall, James. *Borges, A Life.* New York: BasicBooks, 1996.

Further Reading

Borges, Jorge Luis. *A Personal Anthology*. London: Grove/Atlantic, Inc., 1994.

Casares, Adolfo Bioy, and Daniel Martino. *Borges*. Planeta Publishing Corp., 2007 (Spanish-language edition).

Samuels, Steven, and Adrian Lennon. *Jorge Luis Borges: Argentine Writer*. New York: Chelsea House Publishers, 1992.

Strathern, Paul. *Borges in 90 Minutes*. Chicago: Ivan R. Dee, 2006.

WEB SITES

http://www.themodernword.com/borges/
http://www.hup.harvard.edu/features/bortcd/
http://www.sccs.swarthmore.edu/users/00/pwillen1/lit/index3.htm
http://www.literatura.org/Borges/ (Spanish language)
http://www.los-poetas.com/b/borges.htm (Spanish language)

Picture Credits

page:

8: Photo by Horst Tappe/Hulton Archive/Getty Images
11: © Bettmann/Corbis
16: Photo by Sigwart Blum/FPG/Hulton Archive/Getty Images
21: AP Photo
27: Sergio Caro/WpN
31: Sergio Caro/WpN
41: AP Photo
51: © Anthony John West/Corbis
57: Photo by Dmitri Kessel/Time Life Pictures/Getty Images
61: AP Photo/DYN Agency, Marcelo del Arco
71: AP Photo
76: Gisele Freund/Photo Researchers, Inc.
87: © Bettmann/Corbis
91: Photo by Charles H. Phillips/Time Life/Getty Images
96: Photo by Keystone/Getty Images
100: AP Photo/Domenico Stinellis

cover: © The Bridgeman Art Library, London/SuperStock

Index

About the Author

TIM McNEESE is associate professor of history at York College in York, Nebraska, where he is in his seventeenth year of college instruction. McNeese earned an associate of arts degree from York College, a bachelor of arts in history and political science from Harding University, and a master of arts in history from Missouri State University. A prolific author of books for elementary, middle and high school, and college readers, McNeese has published more than 90 books and educational materials over the past 20 years, on subjects ranging from the founding of Jamestown to Spanish painters. His writing has earned him a citation in the library reference work, *Contemporary Authors*, and multiple citations in the reference work, *Best Books for Teen Readers*. In 2006, McNeese appeared on the History Channel program, *Risk Takers, History Makers: John Wesley Powell and the Grand Canyon*. He was a faculty member at the 2006 Tony Hillerman Mystery Writers Conference in Albuquerque, where he presented on the topic of American Indians of the Southwest. His wife, Beverly, is an assistant professor of English at York College. They have two married children, Noah and Summer, and three grandchildren, Ethan, Adrianna, and Finn. Tim and Bev sponsored study trips for college students on the Lewis and Clark Trail in 2003 and 2005 and to the American Southwest in 2008. You may contact Professor McNeese at tdmcneese@york.edu.